CONTENTS

Mervyn Pichel and Neil Curtis

BITING FIT

The patient's guide to
DENTISTRY

γ

GAMMA PUBLISHING · OXFORD

First published in the UK 1986 by Javelin Books as Have Healthy Teeth and Gums.

Published in the UK 1999 by Gamma Publishing Oxford as Teeth and Gums: An Owner's Manual

This revised edition published in the UK 2006 by Gamma Publishing Oxford

ISBN 0-9524594-1-8   978-0-9524594-1-5

A CIP record for this book is available from the British Library

Edited by Neil Curtis Publishing Services

This edition produced by John Saunders Design & Production

Printed and bound in the United Kingdom by Biddles Limited

PREFACE TO THIS REVISED EDITION

Once again there have been many changes in the dental profession since the previous edition of this book. We continue to promote the message that dental disease is largely preventable. At the same time, we must point out that there has been an increase in tooth-enamel erosion among the public at large of almost epidemic proportions. Prevention of malignant disease of the mouth has also been emphasized because, unfortunately, there has been a rise in reported cases of mouth cancers.

Tooth bleaching has certainly arrived in the United Kingdom, and the Botox procedures that are now being used in some dental practices have also been described.

Obesity is increasing rapidly in the general population. Government departments have been asked to legislate on the more complete and accurate labelling of all food products. Indeed, the dental profession has been lobbying for this for decades. Obesity and the increase in tooth decay and gum disease are closely related subjects. Once again, we have emphasized this topic.

ACKNOWLEDGEMENTS

The authors wish to acknowledge the assistance of the following people in producing this book:

The Dental company Claudius Ash has supplied the photographs of one of their dental radiographic machines featured on page 161. We owe thanks to Mr Richard Fieldhouse, Dip. Orth. RCS for allowing us to use study models to produce the photograph number 22.

The General Dental council kindly granted permission for us to quote from the 'Notice for the Guidance of Dentists', November 1981, relating to the administration of sedatives and anaesthetics by dental surgeons.

Hamilton Photographics made the difficult task of photographing X-ray pictures much easier than we could have managed unaided. Our thanks to Mr R Higham of Keen Commercial Photographic for producing the photographs.

Our sincere thanks also to Lawrence Kotlow, DDS for his kind letter of encouragement and for allowing us to refer to his article on breast feeding as it appeared in the *American Journal of Dentistry for Children*, May 1977, pages 192-93. Also from the USA, we thank the American Society for Clinical Nutrition for permission to produce the Comparison Table of Human and Cow's Milk as it appeared in the *American Journal of Clinical Nutrition*, 24 August 1971, page 971, Gyorgy & Paul.

We acknowledge the assistance given to us by the Pharmaceutical Press and the courtesy of Her Majesty's Stationery Office in allowing us to reproduce the 'Steroid Warning Card' (Crown Copyright).

Our thanks also to Dr Pat Chapman for describing the 'Double Mouth Guard' used in contact sports.

We thank Mr John R Richardson LDS, RCS (Eng.) of Birmingham for providing the photographs of patients who have received dental implants.

Many thanks to Dr Iain Mackie for allowing us to reproduce the list of suger-free medicines as it appeared in *Smile* magazine.

Our thanks to Miss A E Welham of Johnson & Johnson Dental Division at Slough, Buckinghamshire for kindly arranging the drawings on tooth brushing. We also thank the photographic department of Johnson & Johnson for their work on our behalf.

To Richard Satherley our grateful thanks for allowing us to use his photograph to show 'a glimpse of the future'.

To Dr S Joyston-Bechal for advising on fluoride supplementation, and Dr A Rugg-Gunn for reading our text on fluoride for the 1999 edition.

Dr Surinder Hundle BDS, L.D.S.R.C.S. (Eng) C/o Lund Osler, Knightsbridge, London, kindly supplied illustrations 13 and 14.

INTRODUCTION

The renowned zoologist and broadcaster, Dr Desmond Morris, stated in his book *Manwatching* that a 'smile was the single most important bonding signal in the entire human gestural repertoire'. The smile is an instinctive response of the newborn infant and endears the baby to its parents. Nature has taken millions of years to develop this instinctive behaviour in the newborn child and therein lies the fact that an attractive, healthy smile is important to our well-being and, it must be said, to the reaction of other people towards us. If one's dentition is neglected and uncared for, for whatever reason, that smile can be marred by unsightly decaying teeth, by infected gums, and even by bad breath.

There is no need for your smile to be marred in this way and, moreover, it is also worth realizing that good dental health is an essential ingredient in maintaining good general health.

'I'm certainly not going back to the dentist again until I have to. I haven't been for ten years and now she tells me that I have to have thirteen fillings.' This records, as accurately as memory will allow, part of a conversation between two young ladies, overheard during the course of a train journey. Sadly, it reflects the fears that 'going to the dentist' still hold for many people despite health education programmes and the advances that have been made in dental science in recent years. Too many people still seem willing to suffer the pain and inconvenience of the loss of some or all of their own teeth by middle age, or even much earlier, either from neglect or an unwillingness to visit the dentist regularly. It is the aim of this book to convince everyone that tooth decay is not an inevitable consequence of normal living and that they, together with their dentist, can do much to ensure that their teeth and gums will stay healthy and look good for most if not all of their lives.

Many of us lavish more attention and money on our motor cars than we are prepared to expend on our teeth. Although it is possible to buy a brand new car, a new mouth cannot easily be purchased – at least, not one that is as good as the one we are born with! Apart from those of the human species, the teeth of most animals last their life-time although, of course, in most cases, this is rather shorter than even the traditional 'three score years and ten' and, in many instances, it is tooth loss or tooth wear that determines the animal's fate when it is no longer able to feed. Ironically, it has been our own ingenuity that has, to some extent, led to the all too common neglect of our teeth. We have been able to cut, prepare, and cook our food so that loss of teeth did not lead to starvation, even before the advent of the aid much loved by the stand-up comic, the denture!

In the wild, animals rely on their teeth for a variety of activities including killing prey, tearing up and masticating all kinds of different food items, defence, locomotion, grooming, and communication through facial expressions. Some animals even use their teeth to hold on to a mate! It is also true that, generally, few animals, apart from ourselves, have access to the kinds of food and drinks, such as sweets, candies and fizzy 'pop', that lead so quickly to tooth decay although every pet owner knows that a dog will soon become addicted to chocolate if it is offered as a treat. On the other hand, animals are obliged to deal with tough grasses or even bones when they eat so their teeth may easily be worn down. But wildlife conservationists would find their task even harder than it is if animals faced tooth decay and gum disease on the same scale as civilized human beings.

It was almost 100 years ago that Arthur Ebbles wrote in the scientific journal, *Nature*, 'There is little doubt that an open air life and healthy surroundings encourage the formation of sound teeth in a sound body; but I cannot but think that the principal cause of caries (tooth decay) must be looked for in the food.' He went on to say that imperfect nutrition during the development of the teeth (i.e. from conception), together with the use of soft cooked foods, provide some of the factors necessary for the process of decay to begin. We consider ourselves to be at the acme of the evolutionary tree and yet, even though science has known much about the care of teeth since the nineteenth century, it has been over only the last twenty-five years or so that public awareness of its importance has been widespread. But still some people seem unable to master the techniques of brushing their teeth, still children are given sweets as a treat rather than nuts or a piece of cheese, and still many are unwilling to visit the dentist and even some that do become hysterical in the waiting room. And so, a century after Arthur Ebbles's article in *Nature*, President Carter of the USA, with the famous 'peanut' smile, found it necessary to write to the American Dental Society for Children, 'Dental health is a priority concern for all nations; as a parent, I know the critical importance of good dental care to the well-being of a child.'

It is encouraging that tooth decay and gum disease are preventable and that, by easy steps, everyone can have a healthy mouth which will stay healthy:

1 Read this book! It will allay many of your fears.
2 Visit your dentist regularly – you may even look forward to the chat!
3 Clean your teeth and gums efficiently with a properly formulated fluoride toothpaste – this book will help you learn how.
4 Work out and stick to a sound and healthy diet – not just for the sake of your teeth and gums!
5 Make sure your children follow these guidelines.
6 Discuss with your dentist how to continue to finance your future dental care, especially during this time of change (*see* Chapter 10)

Perhaps tooth decay and gum disease will one day cease to be two of the commonest diseases in the world.

1 THE MOUTH IN HEALTH

THE HEALTHY SMILE

Some animals, carnivores, eat the flesh of other animals. Carnivores have sharp front teeth for incising and tearing flesh while their back teeth are used for grinding meat and bone. They are immensely strong teeth supported by equally powerful jaws. We have only to look at the fossils of dinosaurs to see the lengths to which nature has gone to develop the 'chewing machine', the dentition.

Other animals feed on vegetation and, although plant-eating animals, the herbivores, are generally less aggressive than carnivores, they also need a well-maintained, powerful chewing machine to cope with chewing grasses and other tough, fibrous plants. If you like, the human dentition is a combination of these two types of 'chewing machine' and, if it is healthy, is very efficient and powerful.

In combination with a sophisticated set of muscles, the teeth, jaws, and lips of the human can also provide that important gesture mentioned in the Introduction, *the smile*. Most psychologists agree that you are more likely to receive a favourable response to a request if you start with a smile. Any magazine editor knows the importance of the attractive, toothy grin on the front cover of a latest publication; next time you go to the newsagent take a look at some of the front covers.

THE TEETH AND JAWS

A house is only as strong as the foundations upon which it is laid and, similarly, the dentition is dependent upon its supporting structures. If we are to understand better how dental disease can occur and how it can be prevented, it is important that we should have a detailed knowledge of the teeth and gums. Therefore, this chapter takes a relatively comprehensive look at the make-up of the teeth, gums, and jaws and, although it is not intended to be a textbook, its approach does include information that is not normally included in standard dental health education publications.

The teeth begin to form in the human embryo within the first weeks after conception when it is only about six weeks old. At this stage, the whole embryo is only about a centimetre (0.4 inch) long. Clearly, much of the nourishment which is required by the developing child comes directly from the mother so that her diet is of great importance if it is to grow healthily. The newly growing teeth are referred to as 'tooth buds' and there are spaces between each one during the life of the foetus. As the teeth develop, so do the jaws, and, at birth, the lower jaw is perfectly shaped with the exception that the pronounced chin region has not yet formed. If you examine a baby's face closely, you will see that the vertical part of the jaw bone is shorter than it is in an adult. As the teeth move through the bone, or erupt, the jaw bone begins to change. The bony arches of the jaws develop and this is stimulated further by suckling and by tongue and lip movements. This is just one of the reasons why some members of the medical and dental professions encourage breast feeding. The teat on an artificial feeder does not work in the same way as a human nipple although a consultant paediatrician has designed a teat which is closer in function to a human nipple than any other feeder currently used.

In all, twenty teeth erupt between the ages of six months and two-and-a-half-years with ten in the upper jaw and ten in the lower. We have mentioned these average dates of eruption, only as a guide. (*See* Table i) The premature appearance of a tooth does not portend advanced development, nor should you think that a delay in the eruption of teeth indicates that the child is backward or underdeveloped. The condition in which teeth are absent altogether is called 'anodontia' and is distressing for child and parent alike. While anodontia is rare, partial anodontia is quite common and, in some adults, the lateral incisor teeth are often absent.

primary teeth
(all present at 2½ years)

Fig. 1 The first of the adult molars appearing behind the last of the primary molars. Note that the first molar (6) of the second dentition appears behind the 'e' of the first dentition. Make sure that your child is aware of the newcomer and remember '6s at six years' – two in the lower jaw and two in the upper jaw.

Table 1 Dates of eruption of the teeth

First teeth
(Sometimes referred to as the milk teeth or deciduous dentition)

There are normally twenty milk teeth – ten in the upper jaw and ten in the lower jaw. The teeth are identified by the first five letters of the alphabet. The ones nearest the mid-line are the a's and those furthest from the mid-line are referred to as the e's. The arrangement is therefore:

$$
\begin{array}{ccccc|ccccc}
e & d & c & b & a & a & b & c & d & e \\
\hline
e & d & c & b & a & a & b & c & d & e
\end{array}
$$

Average dates of eruption
The incisors (a and b) appear in the mouth at about 7 months
The canines (c) appear in the mouth at about 16 to 18 months
First molars (d) appear in the mouth at about 12 to 14 months
Second molars (e) appear in the mouth at about 20 to 30 months

Second teeth
(Sometimes called permanent dentition)

There are normally thirty-two permanent teeth – sixteen in the upper jaw and sixteen in the lower jaw. The teeth are identified by the numbers 1 to 8. The teeth nearest the mid-line of the face are the 1s and those furthest from the mid-line are the 8s.

$$
\begin{array}{cccccccc|cccccccc}
8 & 7 & 6 & 5 & 4 & 3 & 2 & 1 & 1 & 2 & 3 & 4 & 5 & 6 & 7 & 8 \\
\hline
8 & 7 & 6 & 5 & 4 & 3 & 2 & 1 & 1 & 2 & 3 & 4 & 5 & 6 & 7 & 8
\end{array}
$$

Average dates of eruption
Incisors (1 and 2) appear in the mouth uppers 6-8 years
lowers 7-9 years

Canines (3) appear in the mouth uppers 11-12 years
lowers 9-10 years

First and second premolar teeth (4s and 5s) appear in the mouth 10-12 years
First molars (6s) appear in the mouth 6 years
Second molars (7s) appear in the mouth 11-13 years
Third molars (8s) appear in the mouth 17 years and over.

The first teeth are extremely important in establishing the growth patterns in the face although many other factors come into play, too. Thus, it is vital that you make sure your child's first teeth are well cared for because, if they are lost prematurely through decay or accident, this may cause problems of spacing when the second teeth begin to appear. The first of the permanent teeth, conveniently numbered six in the dental arch, normally erupt after the child's sixth birthday (see Figure 1). Make sure you take note of the presence of this tooth and that the child is aware of the newcomer, too. If it is lost, a permanent tooth will not be replaced naturally. The surface of this tooth is often deeply pitted and fissured so that bacteria can lodge here. Between the ages of six and fourteen, the entire first dentition is replaced by a second or permanent set of teeth. The full complement of second teeth numbers thirty-two but this includes the four wisdom teeth, each of which is number eight in each arch, and these do not normally appear until after the eighteenth birthday.

When they are lost naturally, the first teeth literally fall out because their roots resorb and the tooth loses its attachment to the surrounding structures. It is possible that some of their permanent successors may erupt while the first teeth are still present and this may give rise to some concern because the mouth looks so crowded. Dentists refer to this as 'the mixed dentition' stage but, as the first teeth are shed, the situation improves and the child's appearance becomes more acceptable to the anxious parents.

THE MAKE-UP OF A SINGLE TOOTH

For descriptive purposes, the tooth can be divided into three regions: the crown, which is the area above the gum margin and covered by enamel; the neck of the tooth, or cervical region which is located at gum level; and the root of the tooth which is situated in the jaw bones. In addition, each tooth comprises four different structures: enamel; dentine; cementum; and the pulp.

Enamel

The first part of the tooth to appear through the gum is the enamel which is the hardest tissue produced in the human body and covers that part of the tooth above gum level. At the tip of the tooth, the enamel is about 2.5 millimetres ($1/10$ inch) thick and it becomes thinner towards the neck of the tooth at gum level. Everyone knows that the colour of teeth can vary and this is essentially dependent upon the thickness of the enamel (see Figure 2). Where the enamel is thin the underlying dentine (see below), which is a yellowish colour, shows through and the tooth appears to be yellow. At the tip of the

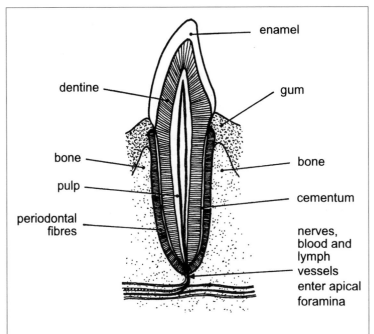

dentine

enamel

gum

bone

bone

pulp

cementum

periodontal
fibres

nerves,
blood and
lymph
vessels
enter apical
foramina

Fig. 2 Diagrammatic section through an incisor tooth and its supporting structures.

tooth where light shines through the enamel, it appears to be an almost bluish-white colour because there is no dentine present at this point. If teeth are very white in colour, it does not necessarily mean that they are any stronger, nor does it suggest that they are more likely to suffer from decay if they are yellowish. Teeth may become stained for a variety of reasons, including from any drugs that a mother may take while she is pregnant, or from those taken during childhood. Even childhood illnesses may affect the appearance of the enamel (*see* Chapter 9).

Enamel is composed of crystals of a chemical substance called calcium hydroxy apatite. Individual crystals are invisible to the naked eye and the actual crystalline structure of enamel can only be observed using a high-powered electron microscope. The following substances are also present in human tooth enamel: sodium, magnesium, carbonates, and phosphates. Interestingly, the surface of the enamel is richer in fluoride than the rest of the tooth. Fluoride (*see* Chapter 2) is known to inhibit the progress of tooth decay and provides valuable additional protection against tooth-decaying acids which form in the mouth, particularly after eating foods that are high in sucrose.

Dentine

Beneath the enamel, making up the main 'body' of the tooth, is the dentine, which is yellowish in colour and not so hard as the enamel. Dentine also contains calcium hydroxy apatite crystals, although these are smaller than those found in the enamel. About three-quarters of the dentine by weight is made up of these crystals, while the rest is referred to as the organic content. Research is still being conducted into the structure of dentine, and it is still not fully understood why it is so sensitive. The organic part of the dentine is produced by special cells called *odontoblasts*. They send out long projections or processes which enter the so-called *dentinal tubules* and it is possible that any variations of temperature and pressure on the teeth initiate painful stimuli in these projections which, in turn, are transmitted to the central nerve in the tooth which lies, with its associated blood vessels, in the pulp canal. The nerves and blood vessels which supply a tooth are branches of the major ones shown in Figure 2.

The pulp

It is these nerves and blood vessels which make up the pulp of the tooth. Inside the pulp canal and pulp chamber, there are also special defence cells which combat infecting bacteria and other micro-organisms. The nerves which supply the pulp are of two types: one type initiates contraction and expansion of the muscle walls of the blood vessels and the other carries the sensation of pain to the brain. Indeed, the only sensation that can be felt within a tooth is pain. The blood vessels, nerves, and branches of the lymphatic system of the body all enter the tooth through tiny holes, called *apical foramina*, at the tip of each tooth root. (*See* Figure 2.)

Cementum

The root of the tooth, which is generally considered to be that part which is not covered by enamel and is surrounded by bone, is attached to the bone via the *cementum* and the *periodontal fibres*. Cementum is similar to bone and is composed of about 70 per cent *inorganic apatite crystals*, together with an organic element that is largely *collagen* (which is a protein found in many parts of the body). From about the second to the eighth decade of a person's life, the cementum probably trebles in thickness. It receives the principal fibres of the periodontal membrane so that the tooth is secured to the surrounding bone. This important area around the tooth is made use of in orthodontic procedures (*see* Chapter 7) which are involved with moving teeth into more favourable positions under mild pressure. Sometimes, there is a tiny collar of cementum above gum level. If you brush your teeth too vigorously, or if you continually eat a diet which is highly abrasive, this collar can be worn away to expose the exquisitely sensitive dentine.

Tooth support

The *periodontal fibres*, which attach the tooth to the surrounding bone, are between 0.1 and 0.33 millimetre thick. They are constantly stressed by the pressures of chewing, but they are continuously repaired and replaced in a healthy mouth. The periodontal fibres attach the teeth to the bone, to the gum tissue and above the crest of bone, between each tooth, from one tooth to another. The latter is referred to as *transeptal fibres*. Periodontal fibres can be destroyed by the toxins produced by the bacteria which normally inhabit all mouths. Therefore, it is extremely important to control the numbers of these bacteria: if the balance tilts in favour of the bacteria, gum disease and tooth decay will follow.

Thus, the root of the tooth is surrounded by bone and admits nerves and blood vessels into the tooth itself. Therefore, a tooth is not an isolated structure but is very much a part of the body as a whole and the loss of even a single tooth should not be accepted with equanimity. Admittedly, losing one tooth is not so devastating as the loss of a major organ but it is certainly not wise to ignore the fact that the second dentition is irreplaceable and that the first dentition is important in establishing facial growth patterns.

Healthy bone in a healthy mouth is covered by a firm, pink layer of stippled tissue, known as the gum, or gingiva, which is bound down tightly to the underlying bone around the necks of the teeth. Beyond this area, it is more loosely attached and, as it approaches the lip region, it is reflected to form a groove, or *sulcus*. When you brush your teeth, you should begin here so that the entire sulcus, gum, and tooth are cleaned effectively. Perhaps the use of the very name 'toothbrush' has been partly responsible for the prevalence of gum disease, and 'tooth/gumbrush' would give a more accurate idea of the task for which the appliance has been designed. The bone which surrounds each tooth is subject to all the pressures that are transmitted through the teeth which can be considerable. The pressure exerted by a human male's bite between his back teeth is some 25 kilograms per square centimetre (360 pounds per square inch) although it is only about half this figure between the front teeth.

It is also important to bear in mind that teeth work only in pairs; that for each upper tooth, there is also a lower. Therefore, if you lose one tooth its counterpart in the opposing dental arch becomes redundant so far as chewing is concerned. Losing only one tooth alters the bite and this can upset the movements of the jaw and perhaps even cause pain in the jaw joints.

The jaws consist of two bony parts. The lower moveable part is the *mandible* and the upper, fixed part is the *maxilla*. To provide maximum chewing efficiency, the upper and lower teeth should interdigitate with one another when the jaws close, as shown in Figure 3. From a side view, you can best see the situation that is referred to as a normal occlusion (closing). Even the tiniest particle of food can be detected by the teeth when they close together so that you can obviously appreciate the very delicate balance at play during chewing. Recent evidence even suggests that some types of migraine can be caused by an interference in the chewing cycle, associated with the loss of teeth or with the wearing away of artificial or natural tooth substance. These imbalances are detected by the nerve endings in the muscles that are concerned with chewing and the tension that is felt in these muscles can cause considerable stress. Therefore, if you are unlucky enough to suffer from migraine, it would be wise to consult your dentist as well as your doctor.

THE JAW JOINT

The maxilla is fixed while the mandible is capable of a wide range of up-and-down, sideways, and backwards-and-forwards movements. Firstly, the lower jaw adapts to its function of carrying the ten milk teeth, and then the sixteen permanent teeth, during the early years of life by modifications in its shape. This is brought about by increase and decrease in density of bone at various sites in the jaw bone. One particular area of growth is the *condyle* region of the lower jaw which also provides part of the mechanism of the jaw joint. A depression in the bone of the upper facial skeleton receives the condyle but is separated from it by a disc of cartilage. The arrangement mimics a ball-and-socket joint in some respects. The disc merges into a fibrous capsule which surrounds the whole joint. The condyle can become damaged in arthritis sufferers. This can be painful and, in some cases, early treatment can be very beneficial (see Figure 4a). Undue pressure can also be brought to bear on the jaw joint by dental irregularities and disease which is yet another reason why you should keep your teeth and gums healthy.

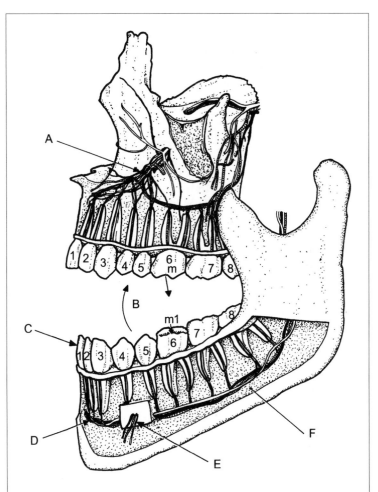

Fig. 3 The chewing machine – how the teeth meet (occlude). When the jaw closes, the lower teeth close behind the upper front teeth. The upper molar cusp 'm' meets the lower molar at 'm1'. This is referred to as the norm or class I occlusion.

A   Blood vessels and nerves supplying the teeth of the upper jaw.
B   Shows the direction of closing. m is the cusp of the upper tooth 6 which engages the groove m 1 in the lower molar 6.
C   The lower incisors touch the backs of upper incisors when jaw is closed.
D   Blood vessels and nerves supplying the teeth of the lower jaw.
E   Mental nerve supplying the chin region.
F   Mandible with bone removed to show the roots of the teeth.

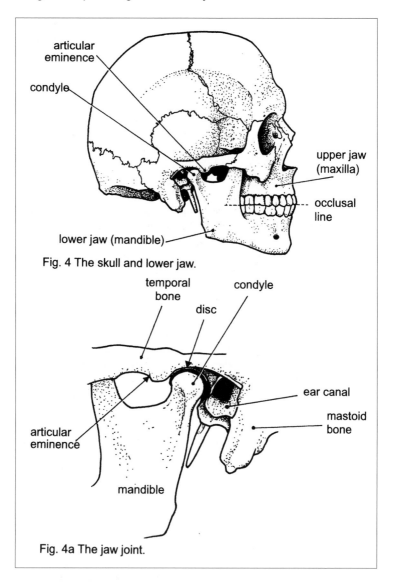

Fig. 4 The skull and lower jaw.

Fig. 4a The jaw joint.

TEETHING TROUBLES

Stories of sleepless nights for parents and children abound, as do the tales of serious illness associated with the appearance of teeth in the mouth. In fact, we could be forgiven for thinking that our teeth bring us nothing but pain from the cradle to the grave. But, to be positive, we should accept that teething is a perfectly natural event evolved to alter the dentition to adapt from breast feeding, to eating solid foods, and drinking. The process does not come to an end until after the third molars have erupted (*see* Chapter 5 and Table 1 for the dates of eruption of teeth) and they, too, may cause discomfort as they appear.

Remember, though, that there is little evidence to suggest that the eruption of teeth causes illness in children. A slightly raised temperature is not uncommon, however, and if this is the case you must seek medical guidance. Never give an infant aspirin-based medicines of any sort without the agreement of a qualified dentist or doctor. There are specially formulated medicines available if the child does have a raised temperature during teething. Teething discomfort can be relieved by applying certain gels to the sore gums and, in some cases, it may be necessary to give the child a drug to induce sleep. On no account should a drug of this kind be prescribed by anyone other than by a medically or dentally qualified practitioner. Some of the teething gels contain an antiseptic as well as a local anaesthetic substance and can be applied using a clean cottonwool bud or even with your finger provided it is scrupulously clean. Recently some flavoured varieties have become available.

When bleary-eyed parents enter a dental surgery begging for help for their teething infants, the above is the only advice that can really be offered, except also to suggest that the child is given something to chew on during the day, such as a cooled teething ring. Teething rusks may also be useful but do make sure they have a SUGAR-FREE, LOW-SALT FORMULATION. When your child is teething, however, it is also worth seeking advice from health visitors and pharmacists. Once the teeth are through, the real dangers are then from food, drink, and accidental trauma.

Many parents are understandably worried that if their child has some abnormality in the first dentition then the second teeth will be the same. In this case, there is no hard and fast rule, and even the absence of milk teeth does not always mean that teeth will be absent from the permanent dentition. The first teeth are obviously smaller than the second teeth and are usually much lighter in colour. So far as resistance to decay is concerned, there are so many factors involved that it would be impossible to predict whether or not a first tooth is more likely to decay than a second. One thing is certain, however: if a high-sucrose diet is eaten, then there is more likelihood of decay occurring.

If the teeth do not meet or occlude, as shown in Figure 3 treatment may be required to correct the malocclusion as it is called. (See Chapter 7.) If the first teeth show any such anomaly, it is rare for orthodontic treatment (a specialized branch of dentistry concerned with straightening teeth in an overcrowded jaw) to be provided. On the other hand, treatment may be given for problems of this kind which occur in the second dentition,. Malocclusion in the first dentition does not mean that the permanent teeth will be affected but, similarly, normal occlusion in the milk teeth does not necessarily indicate freedom from the problem in the second teeth.

Sometimes, the malocclusion results from abnormal bone growth such that the upper teeth appear to be very prominent. In other cases, it is the lower jaw which is overgrown and the upper teeth close behind the lower ones instead of the other way round. All these conditions can be alleviated, if not corrected, with expert guidance from orthodontists.

Parents should be seeking advice about dental care for their future offspring while the mother is pregnant. There is insufficient encouragement for the examination of small infants, and dentists would be prepared to give sound advice to a pregnant woman. Do not wait until your child has problems before seeking dental advice or think that a particular age is correct to begin dental examinations. The mouth should be examined often to establish the presence or absence of diseases, such as thrush in infants and anaemia in the undernourished. Throughout this book, we shall emphasize that we are concerned with the human body as a whole and not only with the teeth.

In the past, invasive treatment of the mouth has always been the domain of medically and dentally qualified personnel. The more recent fashion for tongue piercing and the placing of jewellery in the tongue requires special mention. Anyone considering this procedure should be fully aware that the same stringent cross-infection guidelines followed by dental surgeons should be strictly adhered to by those practising the procedure. This means that all instruments used should be autoclaved (sterilized) before use to the same standard as would be used in dental practice. There has been one reported case of severe infection in the floor of the mouth as a result of this procedure but not necessarily due to inadequate sterilization. The risk, however, is always present that tongue piercing can result in infection long after the insert is placed. The additional risk is that the tongue stud can be dislodged, swallowed, or even more seriously, inhaled. There are cases reported of the presence of the tongue stud being bitten and causing damage to the front teeth. The British Dental Association has been reported to have recommended that tongue piercing is putting not just oral health but general health at risk and strongly advise people not to pursue the practice.

2 PREVENTIVE DENTISTRY

Almost everyone has seen or felt the effects of tooth decay, but it is surprising how few people are aware of how the disease is caused. *The Guinness Book of Records* mentions tooth decay as one of the most prevalent diseases in the world. There are many factors responsible for the start of the process of tooth decay, as well as many that are responsible for the progression of the disease. We list here some of those factors which have a bearing on it. This list is by no means exhaustive as other things may be discovered in the future.

1 Diet (sugar consumption).
2 Plaque (bacterial activity converting sugars into acid).
3 Heredity – shape of teeth; chemistry of tooth enamel; fluoride uptake.
4 Saliva production.
5 Age.
6 Susceptibility of the sexes to decay.

Like many of our other features, the shape of our teeth is largely inherited and controlled by the genes passed on through our parents. Unfortunately, those of us who have been blessed with teeth that have a pitted or irregular surface are more likely to suffer from tooth decay than those whose teeth are smooth, even, and regular. Normally, the surfaces of the molar teeth at the back of the mouth are more uneven and pitted than those of the front teeth, so that they are the ones which are especially likely to undergo attack (*see* Figure 5). This is because these areas are more difficult to keep clean and the bacteria that cause decay can lodge here undisturbed for long periods of time. The contact points between adjacent teeth are vulnerable, too, for the same reason. Many people, then, manage to keep their front teeth in good condition for a greater part of their lives while the back ones may be filled with amalgam, crowned, or replaced by a denture or implant.

As you have already seen, the tooth enamel is the outermost protective covering for the tooth and, once again, its make-up differs from person to person. It is a crystalline material and very tough but the crystal structure of the enamel in one person's teeth may be more resistant to decay than another's. Possibly this may be due to the

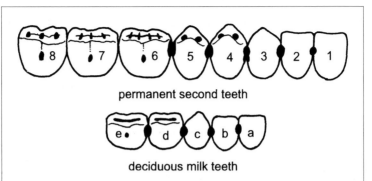

permanent second teeth

deciduous milk teeth

Fig. 5 The danger areas. All shaded areas are prime sites for bacterial plaque to accumulate and cause decay and gum disease.

varying quantities of fluoride in the enamel and, of course, the administration of fluoride has been the subject of much debate for many years. Once again, though, inherited factors may play a part in determining how much fluoride is incorporated into the developing enamel.

Bacteria are microscopic, single-celled living organisms which lack the green pigment chlorophyll and have been described as plants, as animals, or even as some kind of interim stage between. There are many which are harmful and lead to disease while others, such as those that live in the gut of animals including humans, are vital to our very existence. Bacteria reproduce very rapidly so that they can evolve new forms extremely quickly. Indeed, there are even bacteria that feed on the kerosene fuel which aircraft use! Those bacteria that occur naturally in the mouth form colonies on all the surfaces of the teeth and organize themselves on the fine membrane (pellicle) that covers every tooth. Together with mucin, a sticky component of normal saliva, a coating called plaque is formed. As we have explained, this is more difficult to remove from irregular, pitted teeth.

Plaque is very sticky and it is within the plaque that the process of decay begins. Plaque is a natural deposit but it becomes a problem when a diet rich in sugar is eaten because the bacteria in plaque convert the sugar into acids. This is rather like the process of fermentation whereby yeasts convert sugar into alcohol but, unfortunately, the results are rather less pleasant! The acids that are formed in plaque attack the enamel of the teeth and cause it to dissolve. The bacteria then have access to the dentine of the tooth and eventually to the nerve and blood vessel in the pulp canal.

Sugar is an all-embracing word for a variety of different carbohydrates. The one that we most often encounter, such as in normal granulated sugar or in many sweet drinks, is sucrose and, unfortunately, this is the main culprit in the initiation of tooth decay, although all sugars should be thought of as potentially damaging to our teeth. The Inuit of North America provide us with a good living example of the effects of sugar on teeth. Before they began to trade with our culture, Inuit were relatively free from tooth decay but, over recent years, there has been a dramatic increase in its incidence among these people.

Between the ages of six and twenty-one years, the teeth seem to be most vulnerable whereas, later in life, they are less likely to be attacked and the actual process of decay is slower, too. As one grows older, however, it is more likely that teeth will be lost through gum disease rather than through decay.

Most dentists are agreed that the presence of fluoride in the chemical structure of a tooth makes it more resistant to acid attack but, during the formation of the teeth, it takes time for the fluoride to be incorporated. Girls' teeth erupt sooner than those of boys. Because fluoride is taken up during the development of the tooth before it erupts and, because girls' teeth develop more quickly, they take up less fluoride. Therefore, they are more vulnerable to decay. Furthermore, because girls' teeth appear sooner, there is a greater likelihood of their teeth being subjected to acid attack sooner. Sugar consumption is of great importance to the decay process. *It is certainly the frequency with which sugar is eaten rather than the volume consumed which is significant.* The longer sugar is in the mouth, the more time the bacteria have to increase the acid level. Within a few minutes, the acid level increases enough to allow it to begin attacking the enamel. Timing the speed with which acid forms after eating sugar was one of the first important investigations which led to the discovery of how decay takes place.

The first person to carry out these sorts of experiments was R. M. Stephan, so that graphs which show the change in acidity with time after consuming sugar are known as Stephan curves. The graph in Figure 6 plots the pH of the mouth against time in minutes after consuming a 10 per cent glucose solution which is roughly equal to drinking a cup of tea with one spoonful of sugar in it. The pH is a measure of the acidity or alkalinity of a solution and is represented by a series of whole numbers from 1 to 14, with the lower numbers denoting increasing acidity and the higher ones greater alkalinity. A neutral solution has a pH of 7. You can see from the Stephan curve that drinking a sugary solution causes a marked decrease in the pH in

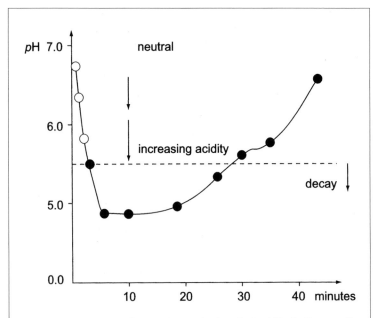

Fig. 6 The Stephan Curve shows the level of acidity in the mouth after ingesting a 10% glucose solution. Note that pH below 7.0 indicates an acid solution and at pH 5.5 human tooth enamel starts to decay. Manufacturers of products such as tooth pastes and chewing gum are using this diagram more commonly in their advertising.

the mouth, indicating that the acidity has increased sharply. It is worth remembering, then, that if the pH in the mouth falls to 5.5 or less, the concentration of acid is high enough for the enamel of human teeth to begin to dissolve.

It is possible to plot a Stephan curve for any food or drink and, for example, you might be surprised to see the effects after chewing an apple. Although chewing an apple, or other tough foods, does exercise the jaws and stimulates salivary flow, it causes the pH in the mouth to fall to as low as 4 which is more than enough acidity to result in the disintegration of the tooth enamel. But encouraging salivary flow by chewing, say, carrots, celery, or chewing gum decreases acidity. This is referred to as the 'buffering capacity' of saliva and it undoubtedly varies from one person to another. Clearly, therefore, vigorous chewing after a high-sugar diet is beneficial but it will not prevent decay and gum disease altogether because food debris is certain to lodge at the contact points between adjacent teeth. You must remove this debris by flossing.

There is one myth concerning the teeth of women which can quickly be dispelled: pregnancy, and the strain which the condition places on the woman's body, do not cause tooth decay, nor is calcium somehow taken from the mother's teeth and given to the developing baby. It is true, though, that some pregnant women may be less careful about diet and, because they may be more tired, they may be more lax in oral hygiene. There is certainly no reason to believe the old saw that a mother loses one tooth for each child! The hormonal changes which take place during pregnancy, however, do make the gums more susceptible to irritation by plaque. The gums can become quite swollen and engorged with numerous blood vessels which readily rupture when the teeth are brushed. But, when plaque formation is controlled, the problem is greatly diminished.

GUM DISEASE

A dirty splinter in your finger causes inflammation which is indicated by redness of the affected area, heat, swelling, and, of course, pain. Plaque lodged between gum and tooth usually produces much the same effect on the gum. If you remove the splinter, your finger may well bleed as the blood vessels, which have increased in number in response to the irritant, rupture. Similarly, when you brush your teeth and gums so that the previously undisturbed plaque is dislodged, your gums may bleed.

If you were to leave a splinter in your finger for a prolonged period, the infective process may cause more pain, and the battle between the bacteria and the blood's own defence cells results in the formation of yellow pus. Should you remove the splinter at this stage, there may be a considerable flow of pus. In the case of diseased gums, gentle pressure on the area affected by gum disease may cause pus to flow. This used to be called *pyorrhoea* (a flow of pus) but, nowadays, it is more usually referred to as *periodontal disease*, that is, disease of the structures which support the teeth.

While it is hard to tolerate the pain caused by a splinter in the finger for very long, it is rare for diseased gums to be painful. Indeed, one of the reasons why gum disease is so dangerous is because it does not cause pain in its early stages and one is not alert to the disease process which is going on inside the mouth. It is worth remembering that the outcome of gum disease is the loss of teeth when the bone and fibres around each tooth are destroyed. Thus, a completely 'undecayed' tooth can be lost through gum disease. The first sign of this is usually bleeding gums after brushing the teeth. In cases where the teeth are not brushed, which sadly is still a common occurrence, patients are only alerted to the fact that gum disease is present when the teeth are already loose. Therefore, at the first sign of bleeding you must consult a dental surgeon. Better still, don't wait for this to occur, but seek advice from a dentist on how to avoid the problem in the first place. *Gum disease is responsible for a greater loss of teeth in people over the age of twenty-one years than tooth decay!*

Periodontal disease can be stopped once it has begun and a recurrence generally only occurs in the presence of uncontrolled plaque. If you do consult your dentist about 'bleeding gums' your dentist will most likely arrange a programme of oral hygiene instruction for you. This may be carried out by the dentist or by a dental hygienist. Even when gum disease is particularly advanced and the condition is complicated by other problems, referral to specialist 'periodontal surgeons' invariably includes a thorough oral hygiene programme. Many cases of advanced gum disease respond so well to good oral hygiene habits that surgery is rarely performed.

The dentist will resort to surgery when defects in the gum caused by the progress of gum disease actually make it difficult for the patient to remove plaque efficiently. Where the gum has become inflamed and swollen, a space will exist between gum and tooth (*see* Figure 7) and this is referred to as a pocket. The depth of the pocket is a measure of the progression of gum disease.

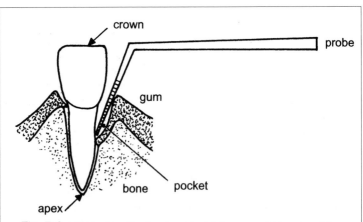

Fig. 7 A measuring device inserted into a pocket caused by plaque. (Note loss of bone and migration of gum towards the root apex.) The graduations are marked in millimetres on the probe.

'Gingivectomy', which means cutting the gum surgically, is the name given to the operation; which seeks to eliminate the pockets that harbour plaque and make its removal more difficult. Where a pocket involves only the soft gum tissue, the defects are generally referred to as 'false pockets'. When the disease process has destroyed bone as well as periodontal fibres, the defects are referred to as *true* or *bony pockets*.

Plaque

Plaque is the main culprit in the progress of gum disease and, indeed, in its initiation so that it is important to remove any factors which make cleaning the teeth more difficult. Tartar (calculus) is calcified plaque. It forms to some extent in everyone's mouth but it appears to be more commonly associated with adults than with children. It seems to form more readily on the tongue side of the lower front teeth, and the cheek side of the upper molars. This is not surprising because it is in these regions that the salivary glands open and pour out their secretions. Thus, any plaque in the area will become *calcified* more easily. (This is the process of hardening by deposition of calcium salts from saliva.) Tartar creates yet another ledge on or under which plaque can form so that still more gum disease will result. This is the main reason why a dentist will recommend that calculus should be removed by scaling. A dental hygienist may carry out this important procedure for you. Calculus which forms below gum level (subgingival calculus) is often quite unsightly because it gives a dark colour to the overlying gum. Therefore, there is often an improvement in the cosmetic appearance of the teeth and gums after a thorough scaling.

Badly fitting partial dentures, or ledgy fillings which snag dental floss, are also plaque traps. Plaque traps in dentures are unwelcome but, provided that the teeth are cleaned scrupulously and the dentures are not worn during sleep, the dentures are acceptable. Photographs 8, 9, 10, and 11 (pages 80–1) show the designs for chrome cobalt 'skeleton' type dentures.

Halitosis

Halitosis (bad breath) is not uncommon even in the healthiest person. Sometimes there are obvious reasons for our breath smelling and being offensive to others – smoking and drinking alcohol are two of the best-known causes. Halitosis tends to increase in old age and may be associated with a decrease in the salivary flow, although this has not been conclusively proved. It can be reduced by rinsing the mouth with chlorhexidine mouthwashes, but this should not exceed two short rinses per day because inflammation of the mucous membranes (cheek, tongue, lip, sulcus) can occur, although this is rare. In any event, this should be carried out only in consultation with your general dental practitioner or medical adviser.

Masking the smell of bad breath with mouthwashes should be carried out with caution. A clean, fresh taste in the mouth does not necessarily mean that the mouth is clean and free from disease. Hiding the smell, as it were, is a little like smothering yourself with perfume without bathing.

Mouthwashes

1 They may contain antibacterial substances that limit the formation of plaque in the mouth.
2 They may be recommended after surgical procedures have been carried out to limit the chances of post-operative infection.
3 They may make you feel better by giving you a fresh-tasting mouth.

In the opinion of the authors, all mouthwashes should be used only with the agreement of a dentist or medical adviser because, if they are used to excess, they may cause irritation to the soft tissues of the mouth. The important thing is to identify the cause of the bad breath. In the absence of digestive problems, lung disease, or even sinusitis, gum disease is a common cause. Thorough mechanical cleaning of the teeth and, in some cases, actually brushing the tongue (without toothpaste) has been known to be beneficial in reducing the strength of the smell. When the problem is caused by gum disease, thorough oral hygiene is the best answer in the long term.

Revealing the plaque

Because plaque is implicated in the progression of tooth decay and gum disease, it would seem obvious indeed that its very formation should be discouraged. Chlorhexidine mouthwashes do control the formation of plaque to some extent. But, as we have already mentioned, they should not be used to excess, so that we must look towards controlling the amount of plaque that is present in our mouths. Remember that plaque forms in all mouths irrespective of diet, but certain diets do make its effects more damaging, and we shall refer constantly to the main offender, sucrose (sugar).

Plaque is white in colour so that it is not easy to see against the white of the enamel. How many people remark, 'But I clean my teeth; why do I have dental problems?' The reason is simply that many areas of the mouth are not cleaned, even by the most scrupulous. The answer to the problem is to see the plaque. This can quite simply be carried out by staining the plaque with a dye. A simple and relatively inexpensive method is to rinse the mouth with a food dye. Rose pink is one that seems to do the job admirably. There are also several brands of 'disclosing tablets' available, but remember that they are to be chewed to release the dye and not swallowed. It is a good idea to smear the lips with petroleum jelly before using the dyes or you may look as though you are wearing lipstick, although this may not necessarily be a problem. Once the plaque is stained, you can then see it clearly and brush it off. Rinsing alone will not achieve this (*see* Figure 10).

Disclosing plaque, then, is very valuable for sighted people but the visually handicapped cannot use this procedure. Therefore, blind people need careful tuition in oral hygiene measures based on detecting the presence of plaque by the tactile sensations of the tongue, together with an awareness of the stagnation areas which are present in the mouth.

To remove plaque effectively from the surfaces of your teeth, you will need to formulate a plan for brushing methodically each area that

Fig. 8 Positioning for brushing the teeth of a small child. (*Left*) Tip child's head backwards to clean upper teeth. (*Right*) Keep child's head straight to clean lower teeth.

is accessible to the toothbrush. The pictures in Figure 9 show a standard method and serve only to illustrate those areas that we consider to be easily accessible to the toothbrush. Your dentist may give you additional advice or, of course, describe a totally different method for you. Every mouth is different and the best method of cleaning is the one which rids your mouth of plaque most efficiently, without damage to the teeth and gums.

Note that some food-colouring dyes contain tartrazine (additive number E102), which is a substance to which some people are allergic. Consult your dentist before using any of the plaque-colouring agents mentioned.

ORAL HYGIENE

Choosing a toothbrush

There is a bewildering array of toothbrushes on the market these days and it is obviously important to choose the type that is the most effective. In fact, the toothbrush was invented more than 200 years ago, in 1780, by William Addis. It is said that he was involved in the Gordon Riots of the time and that, to escape execution, he hid in a slaughterhouse for horses. It was fashionable then to carve pieces of bone and, because there was also plenty of horsehair in his hiding place, he hit

Fig. 9 BRUSH-UP TECHNIQUE. (Courtesy of Miss A. E. Welham Product Manager, Johnson and Johnson Dental Care Division, Slough.)
If you brush your teeth in a disciplined manner, effectively, and with the correct toothbrush, your dental health will be improved. 1 Direct the bristles of your toothbrush towards your gum at an angle of about 45 degrees. 2 Use several short, backwards and forwards strokes to loosen particles of food and bacterial plaque from between the teeth and from the small gap between the base of each tooth. 3 Use several longer brush strokes to carry the debris away from the line of the gum and between the teeth towards the biting and chewing surfaces of the teeth. Brush the chewing surfaces thoroughly. 4 Brush gently on the outside and inside surfaces of each tooth, concentrating on just one or two teeth at a time.

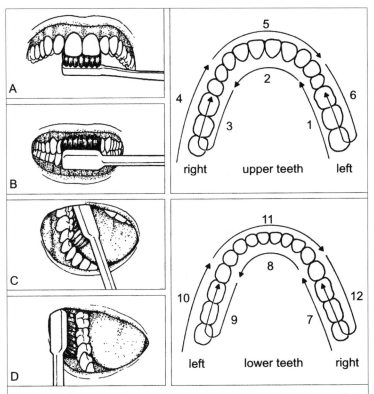

Fig. 9 cont. THE SECTOR BRUSHING ROUTINE. A system for thorough, consistent cleaning.

Diagram A   Brushing front teeth – inside surfaces: 1 Start at the *upper left*. 2 Move to *upper centre*. 3 Then to *upper right*. Finish off with the chewing surfaces of the upper right molars.

Diagram B   Brushing front teeth – outside surfaces: 4 Start at *upper right* 5 Move to *upper centre*. 6 Then to *upper left*. Finish off with the chewing surfaces of the upper left molars.

Diagram C   Brushing back teeth – inside surfaces: 7 Switch to lower jaw and start *lower right*. 8 Move to *lower centre*. 9 Then to *lower left*. Finish off with the chewing surfaces of the lower left molars.

Diagram D   Brushing back teeth – outside surfaces: 10 Start at *lower left*. 11 Move to *lower centre*. 12 Then to *lower right*. Finish off with the chewing surfaces of the lower right molars.

on the idea of inserting the hair into holes in the carved bone and thus he made the first toothbrush. The earliest cleaning aids, however, were probably toothpicks made from twigs, although the Romans

Fig. 10 Plaque displayed (disclosed). Plaque is a white, creamy film which covers the surfaces of the teeth. Under the microscope, it is possible to see the bacteria in the plaque. If you stain the plaque with a harmless food colouring dye, such as rose pink, you will see the plaque on your own teeth.

wrong

correct

Fig. 11 WARNING The correct 'dose' of toothpaste. Don't smother the toothbrush with toothpaste – a small amount, about the size of a pea, is sufficient for children over four years of age. For younger children, just smear some paste (low-fluoride variety) on the brush and supervise all brushing sessions.

certainly fashioned them out of gold. Cleaning the teeth is not the only use to which toothbrushes have been put, and in World War 2 they were made with hollow handles in which maps of Germany, printed on thin paper, could be hidden to assist prisoners of war in their efforts to escape. The first nylon toothbrush came on the market in 1937 but, until then, the brush was made from pig bristle.

When you buy a toothbrush, always choose one that has filaments with rounded tips because this type of brush will not abrade your gums. Make sure, too, that the size of the head is correct for you and for your children. Some manufacturers mark their products to indicate the size of the head, and the size you need will depend in part on the size of your mouth. Remember that a large toothbrush will not clean your teeth and gums any better than a small one, and you should always be able to use it to reach comfortably into the sulcus and to the back of the last tooth in each arch. It is a good idea to buy a small toothbrush for your child as soon as his or her first tooth appears and, at this time, a baby's natural inclination to put everything in the mouth is a useful one to exploit!

Although brushes with natural bristles are still widely available, nylon tufts are much more hygienic, but it is still worth having two brushes so that one can be allowed partly to dry before it is used again.

The toothbrush manufacturers are very alert to methods of capturing the attention of our children, and this is to be encouraged. The use of logos of merchandizable characters on toothbrush handles is very effective in this respect. For example, linking Jurassic Park dinosaurs with dental health is most appropriate as mentioned in the Introduction.

Toothpaste

There seems to be little doubt that using a toothpaste containing fluoride does help to reduce tooth decay, especially in children. Immature enamel does take up some fluoride from the paste and this quite definitely reduces the susceptibility of the teeth to acid attack, although it does not reduce the risk of gum disease. Don't be fooled by the idea that, if you fill your mouth with pleasant-tasting foamy paste with a fresh taste, your mouth is then clean.

Choosing a toothpaste

Do you remember when independent television broadcasting came to the United Kingdom? It was on 22 September 1955, and the first advertisement we saw on our screens was for toothpaste. A tube of toothpaste encased in a large cube of ice extolled the virtues of Gibbs SR as the paste that gave you the tingling fresh feeling when you brushed your teeth. Pepsodent followed with the jingle 'You'll wonder where the yellow went when you brush your teeth with Pepsodent'. In case you have ever wondered what the 'SR' stood for, it was sodium riconoleate, a soap-like cleaning agent.

So what should you expect from a toothpaste? Firstly, it is a cleaning agent. Secondly, it may help prevent tooth decay and gum disease. Thirdly, it may make your mouth taste and feel clean and fresh. And, fourthly, it must not cause any damage to the tissues of the mouth. The major toothpaste manufacturers have the resources to carry out research and to test their products so that they are able to provide accurate clinical data to demonstrate the efficacy of their products.

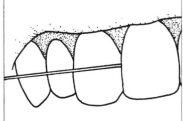

1   Break off about 45 centimetres of floss. Wind one end around the middle finger on your left hand and the other end around the middle finger of your right hand. Leave about 15 centimetres of floss between the fingers. Pull the floss tight. Place the thumbs and forefingers of both hands on the floss leaving 5 centimetres of floss.

2   Gently slip the floss into the gap between two teeth (one hand has partly to enter the mouth to do this). Concentrating on one edge of the tooth, curve the floss into a C shape around it.

3   Slide the floss up the edge of the tooth to the gum. Gently guide it into the natural space between the gum and the tooth.

Fig. 12 Flossing your teeth.

4   Keep the C shape and slide the floss back to the biting surface. Carry the floss to the edge of the adjacent tooth and repeat the procedure. Remove the floss from the tooth gap and repeat steps 1 to 3 for the other gaps between your teeth, giving special attention to your back teeth. As the floss becomes soiled, wind on to some fresh floss and carry on flossing.

Dental floss and tape

Conventional toothbrushes do not penetrate between the teeth. In a normal adult dentition of thirty-two teeth, there are thirty contact points between adjacent teeth and the surfaces below these points are almost inaccessible to brush and paste and they are only reached by chance. The best way to remove plaque which lodges on these surfaces is to use dental floss (*see* Figure 12) which is a fine thread that can pass easily between the teeth. People commonly complain that floss snags on ledgy fillings between the teeth and that they are frightened of dislodging one. In fact, it is useful in itself to discover whether or not you have any ledgy fillings because these should then be replaced by your dentist or, at least, polished using a special strip. If you do find ledgy fillings and these are then smoothed out, you will have reduced the number of potential plaque traps and this aids plaque control. You should also take note if the floss is stained with blood or pus, or if it smells because this is also a sign of gum disease.

Some types of floss are impregnated with a mint flavouring or with fluoride, but remember that the main function of the thread is to remove plaque mechanically. Despite careful brushing and flossing, there are certain areas in some people's mouths that are never cleaned thoroughly. If the mouth is crowded, for example, so that the teeth overlap, they are difficult to clean and, in this case, an interspace brush (*see* Figure 13), which can be bought at most pharmacists, comes into its own. Its small, tufted head is able to reach into the awkward places and the plaque can be removed more easily.

Fig. 13 The interspace brush is useful for cleaning awkward spaces and where there is untreated crowding of the teeth, or around fixed orthodontic appliances.

Other oral hygiene aids

Electric toothbrushes are ideal aids for physically handicapped people – those who suffer from rheumatism or arthritis, for example. The precise movements of the head of an electric toothbrush do help to remove plaque and stimulate the gums. Electric toothbrushes are not cheap but their novelty value may be useful in persuading children to look after their oral hygiene.

Another useful piece of home dental equipment which is available is the water jet which can be used for irrigating the mouth and removing particles of debris that lodge in awkward places, such as between the teeth and under fixed bridges, etc. Basically, the instrument is used, perhaps twice a day, to direct a jet of water, at a frequency of about 1,200 cycles per minute, to flush out food debris from between the teeth that may be difficult to remove by brushing and flossing. It is not, however, a substitute for the toothbrush and should never be considered as such. If you use this piece of equipment incorrectly, food debris can be forced into a pocket which may in itself cause an abscess to develop. It is always wise to seek professional advice before using this appliance, especially if you have ever suffered from rheumatic fever or any of the other conditions that we mention in Chapter 9. The jet of water can perhaps cause bacteria to enter the blood vessels around the gum and teeth. On the other hand, there is no evidence to suggest that these high-pressure water devices can cause damage to teeth or to filling materials.

If your teeth have wide spaces between them, the accessible surfaces can be cleaned by using strips of J-cloth about 8-10 cm long and about 1.5 cm wide. The material is quite absorbent and cleans the wider surfaces more easily than a fine strand of dental floss. It is especially useful when teeth have migrated out of their natural position because of the premature loss of other teeth. If the contact points between your adjacent teeth are adequate, then food debris should not shred between the teeth. If, however, you are constantly irritated by this problem then you should seek dental advice.

PROTECTING TOOTH SURFACES

As we have explained, the teeth most commonly damaged by the decay process are the molars at the back of the mouth. It is an oversimplification to say that these teeth decay because they have uneven surfaces but most would accept that they are difficult to clean properly without correct tuition. To protect the surfaces of these teeth, they can be sealed with a type of plastic coating. The surface of the enamel is etched with a very mild acid which is washed away after it has remained in contact with the teeth for about 30 seconds. A liquid plastic material is then applied to the tooth from a dropper, or sometimes painted on with a fine brush. This is then hardened (polymerized) with a light source (which is often intensified) and the effect is to seal the tiny pits and fissures on the surfaces of the teeth so that

Fig. 14 Fissure sealing may be carried out on molars and premolars in both the first and second dentitions. Note that it provides protection against acids which would otherwise attack the enamel but it does not limit gum disease; nor does it protect any other surfaces apart from those biting (occlusal) surfaces shown.
(Left) Cross-section through molar showing deep groove 'fissure'.
(Right) Sealant in 'fissure' protecting against acid from plaque.

they are shielded from the plaque. In this way, a child's first permanent teeth can be protected when they appear, at the age of about six years, followed by a second treatment of the remaining molars at about twelve years of age. The treatment does not shield the areas between the teeth, where decay can also begin, and fluoride gels or rinses may be used in conjunction with this method.

FLUORIDE

It has been proven conclusively, by statistical evidence in the USA, and from a survey carried out in Birmingham, UK, that, if fluoride is added to drinking water, the incidence of dental decay among those who drink the water from an early age really does decrease. It would seem that, in taking up fluoride, the enamel becomes less soluble in acid so that the activity of the plaque bacteria is less damaging. There is some evidence, too, that fluoride reduces the acid-producing capacity of the bacteria. It has even been shown that, in the presence of fluoride and saliva, the tooth enamel actually remineralizes so that tooth decay is arrested.

It is true that the amount of decay that occurs among people of different age groups, who live in areas where the water is fluoridated, varies but this can be partly explained by the fact that, if fluoride is available during the formation of the teeth, maximum protection is afforded. Fluoride also has a localized effect on the enamel of the teeth. It is this factor which has led to the development of various gels and rinses which can be applied topically to the teeth. The advent of fluoride toothpaste has had a most beneficial effect on the health of our children's teeth. Let us now look at the ways in which fluoride can be administered.

Systemic application

This is the name given to the ingestion of fluoride from a fluoridated water supply, fluoridated milk, salt, tablets, or drops.

It cannot be stressed too strongly that there is not a single shred of plausible evidence to link the fluoridation of water at a level of about one part or lower fluoride per million parts of water with the incidence of cancer. This aspect of water fluoridation has received a good deal of public airing. Both the Royal College of Surgeons and the British Dental Association are quite emphatic on the benefits of water fluoridation at this level and equally emphatic about the absence of risk to those who use the water.

Water fluoridation is, however, a political 'hot potato' and, in a democratic society, a vociferous minority can seem to have as much influence as a silent majority. As a result, the fifty-year-old debate about fluoridation continues. At the moment, about one in eleven persons in the United Kingdom receives water from a fluoridated supply. As the water companies are required to provide wholesome water, it would seem to be advisable to add to the water those substances which have been definitely proven to be beneficial. Fortunately, some water has a natural fluoride component so that the controversy concerning its administration to water supplies has not, at least, deprived some people from the benefits of this substance.

There is an impressive amount of information and scientific evidence which extols the use of milk as a vehicle for fluoride administration. It would appear that, although the fluoride becomes bound to the calcium in the milk, there is still enough available to reduce tooth decay, and almost all the fluoride in milk is absorbed into the body. Fluoridating milk has some other major disadvantages, however. Firstly, it is extremely costly compared to water fluoridation. Secondly, it puts an onus on parents to make sure their children drink such milk. Thirdly, as a 'school milk programme' it will omit all those children under five. Finally, and perhaps equally importantly, not everyone likes milk and there are now very few milk programmes! Nevertheless, it may be very useful in other countries, particularly in its dried form.

Although we have included fluoride tablets and fluoride drops under systemic administration, like fluoridated water, the tablets also have a local effect when they dissolve in the mouth. It must be emphasized that the use of fluoride drops or tablets should only be made after careful consultation with your dentist or medical practitioner, and that additional advice should be obtained from the local water company and district health authority (in the United Kingdom). In other countries, you should obviously consult similar organizations and individuals. *Only if there is less than 0.7 parts of fluoride per million of water in the water supply, is it considered safe to administer any supplement,* e.g. tablets or drops, *and then only in consultation with your dentist.*

Please remember that different parts of the UK have different water suppliers. Indeed, at times of high water demand or when supplies are switched during times of drought, an individual household can receive water with fluoride levels that vary widely between 0 and 1 ppm. If you are going away on holiday or sending your children away to school, you should monitor any fluoride supplementation very carefully.

Children over the age of two years should be encouraged to let the fluoride tablets dissolve slowly, and there is some evidence to suggest that, in the presence of a good salivary flow, remineralization of decaying areas can begin. Fluoridation by 'liquid drops' is not thought to be beneficial for infants under six months old. And now, it is also being recommended that fluoride supplements – drops or tablets – are not essential where fluoride toothpaste is generally used and, of course, not used where there is fluoride in the drinking water. As there is now some indication that slight mottling of the enamel of our children's teeth is occurring in some quarters, it would be wise perhaps to limit fluoride supplementation until after the infant is six months old. The administration of fluoride tablets to pregnant mothers does not seem to offer any advantage to the developing child so that it cannot be considered advantageous to take fluoride systemically during pregnancy.

Bottled 'mineral' water – a warning

This topic was not included in the first edition of this book but, now that more and more people, are drinking bottled water, it has become extremely important and deserves special emphasis. Bottled 'mineral' waters are widely available and can be purchased with no difficulty. Mineral water can even be brought to your door with the daily 'pinta'. The labels do not always offer advice on the fluoride level of the water. One report has suggested that bottlers may have underestimated the level of fluoride in their waters by as much as eight times! Bearing in mind that baby foods, for example, are sometimes mixed with bottled water, this situation must be addressed to avoid the risk of overdosing with fluoride. The labels on bottled waters should carry specific information on the level of fluoride content and it would be sensible to consult your dentist before you drink bottled water as a matter of routine; this is particularly important if you also have a fluoridated tap-water supply.

1 Please remember that there is no such thing as a truly child-proof container. Keep all medicines out of the reach of children.
2 Because it has been proven that some fluoride is good, it does not mean that more fluoride is better. Adhere to the recommended dose. Always seek advice before taking fluoride supplements. If you are using a fluoride toothpaste and there is fluoride in the water supply, there may be nothing to be gained by taking fluoride supplements.
3 At the time of writing, levels of fluoride in water and recommendations for fluoride supplementation are under review so the best policy is to consult your dentist.

Topical application

Avoid using fluoride rinses for children under the age of six years. They are also unnecessary if fluoride tablets are allowed to dissolve in the mouth. Daily rinsing does seem to confer an increased resistance to decay than weekly or fortnightly rinsing but, again, we must emphasize that self-prescription is unwise and you should certainly consult a dental surgeon before embarking on such a course.

The manufacturers of fluoride gels have flavoured their products so that children accept their application more readily. In the light of present knowledge, perhaps this is unwise because a child may well swallow something that tastes pleasantly by reflex action. The dentist or hygienist places the gel in a preformed container – called a tray – that conforms to the U-shaped dental arches so that the gel is applied to the surfaces of the teeth. This method can be used for both the upper and the lower jaws and the gel is allowed to remain in contact with the teeth for about four minutes. The idea is that the free fluoride in the gel leaches out and is attracted to the surface enamel imparting an increased resistance to decay. It is likely that, in the presence of saliva, early demineralization of the enamel is halted and remineralization begins. This procedure is not recommended for children under the age of six years whether it is carried out at home or in the surgery.

Fluoride toothpaste

In 1970 only 5 per cent of the toothpaste sold in the United Kingdom contained additional fluoride. By 1978, the figure had risen to 97 per cent. Young children may swallow quite large amounts of fluoride toothpaste, and some products contain substantial quantities of fluoride. The recommended amount of toothpaste to be used is about 0.3 gram which is about the size of a small pea (*see* Figure 11). But, for children under four years old, just smear the brush with a low-fluoride paste and supervise brushing.

Overdosage of fluoride supplements is rare but, if you do ingest too much, then you should seek medical or dental advice straight away. Drinking copious quantities of milk will be beneficial but it may be that you will need a gastric lavage (stomach washout). Once again, keep all medicines out of the reach of children.

PROTECTING THE TEETH AND GUMS

The teeth and jaws are often damaged in road traffic accidents and the treatment required for injuries of this kind can be extensive. Consequently, we can only welcome the compulsory wearing of seat belts for the driver and front and back seat passengers of all vehicles, as well as the use of 'full face' crash helmets for motor cyclists. Indeed, we must be thankful that there has not been an overwhelming opposition to these measures by those people who feel that this is yet another invasion of personal freedom. Airbags, too, would seem to offer further protection from damage to the teeth and jaws but, in the light of recent accidents, it would seem sensible to add another voice to the pleas for seat belts in all passenger-carrying vehicles such as minibuses, buses, and coaches.

It is not only in motor accidents that the teeth and jaws can be injured, and the face should be protected if you partake in a variety of sports.

Gumshields and mouthguards

There is a risk of injuries to the body in all contact sports such as boxing, rugby, hockey, and basket ball. And, for many years, participants in sports such as these have included gumshields or mouthguards in their equipment. As well as damaging the teeth and jaws, the impact of a blow to the chin can be transmitted to the skull and cause concussion. A gumshield has a cushioning effect, it is very cheap to make, and rarely involves more than two visits to the dentist to have one properly made and fitted. They are not available under the UK National Health Service and, although they can be purchased by mail order, they should always be made and fitted by a dental surgeon. They really are well worth the small cost and inconvenience involved.

The traditional standard gumshield fits only the upper teeth thereby protecting those teeth, their supporting bone, and, to some extent, it cushions the effect of an impact to the chin because the lower teeth will not now crash into the unprotected upper teeth which could result in damage to the back teeth of either jaw. Another advantage is that any force transmitted to jaw joints on either side is diminished and thus the risk of injury to the base of the skull and to the brain is reduced.

In 1984 a new device known as a bimaxillary mouthguard was designed (the lower jaw, usually known as the mandible, was once called the lower maxilla). This mouthguard covers the lower teeth as well as the upper teeth, keeps the mouth open, and maintains the lower jaw in a immobilized position. It was worn by about thirty Australian rugby internationals (all bar one are forwards, including Mr Brendan Nasser who worked on the project with the designer, Dr Chapman). The bimaxillary mouthguard provides more protection than a standard (upper) gumshield, that is:

1 improved protection of teeth of both jaws;
2 the upper and lower jaws are held open at approximately 1 centimetre to provide a breathing space at the front, and consequently there is greater reduction in the force transmitted to the skull, therefore further reducing the risk of concussion;
3 finally, because the lower jaw is now stabilized to the skull, the chance of sustaining a fractured lower jaw is significantly reduced. The standard mouthguard by contrast provides virtually no protection against this, therefore, the bimaxillary mouthguard is ideal for a player returning to competition following a fracture of the lower jaw.

We are indebted to Mr Brendan Nasser BDSc for bringing this information to our attention. It is particularly interesting to note that Brendan Nasser has represented Australia in many international rugby matches and, as a qualified dentist himself, he has literally tested the bimaxillary mouthguard in the field!

Obviously, the appliance costs money to make and its production and fitting require considerable expertise from dental technician and dentist alike. It is perhaps more suitable for use by adults when their dentition is established and the jaws have stopped growing but it is possible to provide protection for the younger sports person provided that it is understood that the appliance may need to be changed as the youngster grows.

Finally, the bimaxillary mouthguard does not replace the standard mouthguard – it is an option for any player but particularly recommended for increased protection in the higher grades of rugby (namely the forwards) where the incidence of injury is greatest, and boxing. It is also recommended for athletes returning to contact sports after sustaining a fracture of the lower jaw.

Industrial hazards

People who work in certain industries where acidic chemicals are used, such as in the manufacture of batteries or lead/acid accumulators, may also risk dental damage. In most factories there are strict precautions to avoid this, but do remember that acid fumes in the environment can actually dissolve in the saliva so that the mouth's acidity is increased (*see* page 28). We may wonder if acid rain affects the teeth!

There are other industries, too, in which the environment may affect the teeth and gums. For example, fluoride is contained in bauxite, which is the raw material used in the production of aluminium. Thus, anyone who works in the aluminium industry may be subjected to higher levels of fluoride than is beneficial and, rather than further reducing tooth decay, overdosing with fluoride actually leads to an unsightly mottling of the tooth enamel. If the metal, selenium, is present in teeth to a high level, they are more prone to decay. Consequently, anyone living in areas close to industrial plants which produce these and other hazardous substances are at risk and it is important that the levels of these chemicals in the atmosphere should be carefully monitored.

In addition to ensuring that precautions are taken to reduce the levels of dangerous substances to which workers are exposed, including wearing masks to avoid inhaling toxic chemicals, factories should provide facilities to help people keep their teeth free from attacks from potentially damaging chemicals. In such industries, every worker should be given the opportunity to be able to rinse the mouth frequently and brush the teeth and gums.

Vaccination

It has been reported that active immunization against tooth decay has been successful in rodents and in non-human primates. Now, trials are about to begin on human subjects. The success of the immunization programme is the culmination of years of research and anti-tooth-decay vaccination may one day become available. Research continues, however, for the bacteria and fungi which actively cause gum disease. They have not yet been positively identified and, until they have, immunization against this particularly damaging dental disorder is not possible.

Initial immunity only against dental disease is passed naturally from mother to child from the placenta during pregnancy, and from breast milk.

Together with these natural defences, the boost of a vaccine against dental disease may bring an end to tooth decay. But, the introduction of vaccination, fluoridation, and thorough cleaning of the teeth and gums should not be thought of as an invitation to consume large quantities of sugar. Sugar is also responsible for other ills, and a leading nutritionist, Professor John Yudkin, has written a book entitled *Pure White and Deadly* (no longer in print but available in some libraries) warning against the hazards of eating refined sugar. We should all try to reduce our consumption of sugar in biscuits, cakes, ice creams, and sauces.

DIET

In a world in which millions of people are starving while those who are fortunate enough to live in affluent societies have more than enough to eat, it is salutary that the commonest diseases are caused by eating the wrong foods. It has been said that 'you are what you eat' and certainly diet and good health are inseparably associated. Such ills as heart and bowel disease, as well as tooth and gum disease, are caused or, at least, exacerbated by eating incorrectly. There is not a perfect way to eliminate sugar from our diet but the amount we eat and its effects can be minimized with a little thought. We are constantly being bombarded with suggestions about the best kinds of foods to eat to ensure sound teeth in a healthy body but it is as well to remember that new research may modify any advice given currently.

'An apple a day keeps the doctor away.' There may be some truth in this maxim but apples do contain natural acids and, if these are allowed to remain in the mouth, they are potentially damaging to the teeth. On the other hand, simply chewing tough, fibrous foods, such as apples, which exercises the jaws and face muscles as well as promoting the production of saliva, is more beneficial than allowing soft, sugary foods to represent the bulk of the diet. Saliva, after all, does have a neutralizing affect on acids. But, although it is impossible to avoid some changes in the acidity of your mouth no matter how carefully you choose your diet, eating apples frequently can no longer be recommended for dental health.

It is very difficult to suggest the 'perfect' diet for everyone, particularly when tastes vary from person to person and when culture and environment dictate what can be eaten. There is, however, one food about which there can be little or no argument and which is freely available to every baby – breast milk. An infant should be breast fed if it is at all possible for it is good for mother and baby alike. The mother benefits from the satisfaction of nursing her own child and, in addition, her body produces a hormone during lactation which causes her uterus to contract so that her body resumes its normal proportions. The baby, of course, receives a natural and correctly balanced diet but also takes in cells from the mother which may in turn affect the type of bacteria present in the infant's mouth. In this way, the mother passes on to her child some immunity to infection.

We have already mentioned how well the human nipple is designed to develop the correct sucking action in babies, while certain bottle-fed infants may be at a disadvantage. In any case, a baby's teeth should not be constantly bathed in any kind of milk and babies should be prevented from suckling for prolonged periods. Human milk contains milk sugar (lactose) and this can certainly damage newly erupted teeth so that, if a child is breast fed after the teeth have erupted, their smooth surfaces can decay. If the child must be bottle fed, you should not add sugar to the feed and, whether the baby is breast or bottle fed, afterwards you should always wipe any teeth that have erupted to remove any traces of food.

Breast milk is, in fact, quite sweet anyway and it seems likely that a taste for sweet foods, associated with the comfort of suckling, leads many adults to eat sweeter foods during times of stress. This may be true during pregnancy, and it is well known that heavy smokers trying to break the habit often resort to sucking peppermints or indulging in other highly sweetened foods. Nowadays, there is definite evidence to suggest that breast feeding is becoming more popular and this is certainly contributing to the reduction in tooth decay among children.

It is interesting to compare the composition of cow's milk and human breast milk (see over).

In view of the fact that breast feeding is increasing in popularity, mothers should be made aware that prolonged suckling of infants can cause damage to their teeth. The lactose in the milk can cause damage to the newly erupted teeth. If children are suckled naturally beyond the teething stage there should be thorough cleaning of the teeth both before and afterwards. The infant should also be suckled in a semi-upright position. This should encourage the flow of milk away from the teeth and therefore swallowed by the infant. Tooth decay actually caused by human breast milk is obviously alarming but it is only prolonged and incorrect feeding that causes this effect. In no way do we wish to discourage breast feeding in favour of bottle feeding. (We are indebted to Dr L. Kotlow for permission to refer to his article in the *American Journal of Dentistry for Children*, May 1977 (pages 192–93).

	Human Milk	Cow's Milk
COMPOSITION		
water/100 ml	87.1	87.3
energy kcal	75	69
TOTAL SOLIDS %		
protein	1.1	3.3
fat	4.5	37
lactose (sugar)	6.8	4.8
ash	0.21	0.72
PROTEINS % TOTAL		
casein	40	82
whey protein	60	18
ASH, MAJOR COMPOUNDS		
calcium, mg	340	1250
phosphates, mg	140	960
VITAMINS IN MG PER LITRE		
vitamin A	1898	1025
thiamine	160	440
riboflavin	360	1750
niacin	1470	940
vitamin C, mg	43	11
REACTION	ALKALINE	ACID

(Courtesy of the *American Journal of Clinical Nutrition*, 24 August 1971, page 971, Gyorgy & Paul.)

From the table it is easy to see that there are substantial differences between the two kinds of milk. Human milk contains more lactose than cow's milk and it is perhaps because of this that sucrose is so often added to a feeding bottle. Obviously, too, a growing calf needs a great deal more calcium than a human baby. Whichever way you choose to feed your baby, beware of overfeeding – you may be bringing up a 'bonny' child but it may not be a healthy one.

The first introduction your child will have to sucrose, which may damage its teeth, is in the sugar that is added to dried milk formulas. Therefore, after consulting your doctor, it is a good idea to reduce or even avoid sugar altogether.

Babies should not require extra sugar and, if they do take it, it does them harm rather than good in the long term. Indeed, the liking for sweet foods begins at this time or is at least heightened by the action. Most parents begin to give their baby a mixed feed when it is about six months old and, at this age, the infant does require extra nutriments. Again, however, you might be tempted to feed highly sweetened foods particularly when the child is teething. But do be careful when you are feeding proprietary foods because many of them are sweetened and some contain as much as 39 per cent more sugar than others. During teething the baby can benefit from chewing on a hard rusk, but some of these are also sweetened and should be avoided. Gnawing on rusks probably stimulates the circulation in and around the mouth, and the saliva flow is increased, which will neutralize any acids in the mouth that have been produced by the plaque bacteria. Some rusks contain extra calcium, iron, and vitamins A and D. Don't forget that plaque can form in the mouth of a child who has not been fed at all, so that even the first two teeth can be coated in plaque if care is not taken.

Children are comforted by the sensation of suckling at the breast so that artificial teats or comforters have become popular. It is tempting for the parent to 'improve' the comforting effects of the artificial teat by dipping it in syrupy liquids, particularly when many of the proprietary kinds offer the advantage of extra vitamins. Certainly, the vitamins are valuable but they need not be taken as a sweet, sticky medicine which will result in tooth decay. It is unwise to soak a comforter in any sweet substance. Rosehip syrup seems to be a popular choice for this purpose, particularly as it is a very rich source of vitamin C, but it is much better to provide it as a drink and then clean your child's teeth afterwards. Solid baby foods may be labelled 'no added sugar' but please do not forget that, like some fruit drinks, many baby foods contain natural sugars so they should not be allowed to bathe a child's teeth for prolonged periods.

If you have already begun to reward your child with sweets, it is not easy to stop it suddenly, so it is best never to start the practice. You would be better advised to offer other foods, such as nuts which, although they can be expensive, are quite nourishing. But, if your child has been rewarded in this way, do reduce the amount of sweet snacks and wean him or her on to more savoury things.

When your offspring first goes to school, you clearly have less opportunity to guide his/her dental hygiene habits but there still remains a good deal that you can do. You should give your child a toothbrush to take to school so that he/she can brush his teeth after any mid-morning snack or after school lunch. Toothbrushes can be bought in small handy containers and even adults should be able to carry one to use at work. Encourage your child to finish the meal with a drink of fresh water and then to brush his/her teeth.

It may not be a good idea to eliminate sugar from the diet entirely but do remember that it is the frequency of eating sugar, rather than the amount consumed, which is damaging to the teeth. We should like to see all manufacturers marking the dangers of sugar on the containers and supermarkets removing the gondolas of sweets from the checkout areas. Certain mineral drinks are especially acidic and you should be very wary of when and how much of these that you or your children consume. Carbonated, fruit-flavoured drinks are particularly lethal cocktails to encourage tooth decay. Although fruit and nuts are less likely to cause dental caries than manufactured foods, and their fibrous nature does have slight cleansing effect, eating them in preference to sweets and biscuits is still not sufficient on its own to avoid tooth decay and gum disease.

Medicines, hidden sugars, and tooth decay

Some medicines contain large amounts of sugar. As we have explained throughout this book, sugars cause tooth decay and, even when we or our children are ill, it seems pointless to use a treatment for one disorder that may well then cause another. There is no need to administer doses of sucrose-laden medicines. One report suggested that some medicines are so sweet that they may contain as much as 60 per cent sugar. Medicines are often taken last thing at night and, if they have a high sugar content, they can be particularly harmful. During sleep the flow of saliva is reduced so that the body's normal defence mechanism against acid attack in the mouth is diminished. Even if you rinse out the mouth after taking a sugary medicine, the syrup will still stick to the teeth and lodge between them and on their surface fissures. The best policy is to ask your doctor, dentist, or pharmacist for sugar-free medication – there is certainly no evidence that the therapeutic value of the medicine is in any way reduced if it is in a sugar-free medium although, in some cases, the active ingredients may be different. Below we have included a list of sugar-free medicines. It is not exhaustive but it does include some products that are available over the counter as well as prescription medicines.

Because tea contains a rather rich source of the proven decay fighter, fluoride, it seems ironic that some people saturate each cup with the proven agent of decay, sugar. Leave it out – it's better for your figure, too.

Many baby food manufacturers are now producing feeds which

Sugar-containing medicine	Sugar-free medicine
Analgesics (pain relief)	
Calpol	Calpol Sugar Free
	Cupanol Under 6 and Over 6
	Junior Disprol
Antihistamines (for allergies)	
Piriton syrup	Phenergan
	Q-Mazine
	Allereze Elixir
	Tavegil Elixir
	Triludan Suspension
Multivitamins	
Abidec	Haliborange Liquid
	Adexolin
Cough preparations	
Actifed Compound Linctus	Junior Meltus Dry Cough Linctus
	Dimotane Co Elixir
	Dimotane Co Paed Elixir
	Expulin Cough Linctus
	Expulin Paed Linctus
Actifed Expectorant	Robitussin Plus
Sudafed Expectorant	Robitussin Plus
Benylin Chesty Cough	Bronalin Expectorant Linctus
	Robitussin Expectorant
Benylin Childrens	Benylin Childrens Sugar-Free
	Bronalin Paed Linctus
	Actifed Cough Relief, Children's
Benylin Dry Cough	Robitussin Junior
Pholcodine Linctus	Galenphol Linctus
Decongestants	
Sudafed Elixir	Galpseud Linctus
Actifed Syrup	Dimotapp Elixir
	Dimotapp Paed Elixir
	Expurhin Paed Elixir

Reproduced courtesy of Dr Iain Mackie and *Smile* magazine.

contain less sugar but, still, none at all is better. Rusks are often liberally coated with sugar and, for the present, it is wise to take note of those products which contain the least.

Out of interest, we have listed here some of the foodstuffs which contain sugar that may surprise you. This information is drawn from the labels on the packaging:

Baked beans
Drinking chocolate
Lemon 'cold relief' powders
Mustard
Salad cream
Canned spaghetti
Tomato ketchup
frozen peas
fish fingers
frozen vegeburgers

Low sugar and sugar-free

It is now possible to buy sugar-free sweets that use artificial sweeteners. Because there is no sucrose in these products, they are far less likely to cause tooth decay if at all. Remember, though, that a label bearing the words 'no added sugar' does not mean that there is no sugar in the product so, once again, always read the information on labels or packaging. For instance, most fruit drinks contain natural fruit sugars and these are harmful to teeth. In Britain, this problem is being addressed, too, so who knows, perhaps we may yet see dentists handing out (sugar-free) sweets to patients?

Artificial sweeteners – sugar substitutes

Firstly, it is not as yet considered entirely safe to administer artificial sweeteners to baby foods. 'Xylitol', for instance, has been reported to cause diarrhoea so it is clearly unsafe for small infants – and not too pleasant for the rest of us either! Xylitol has now been included, however, in a chewing gum. 'Aspartame', most commonly known under the brand name of Nutrasweet, which is widely used in the United States and is now available in the United Kingdom, is unsafe if taken by anyone suffering from the disease phenylketonuria. Any artificial sweetener should therefore be treated with great caution and respect. Obviously, these substances are tested before they are introduced on to the market but constant vigilance is essential to avoid tragedies.

Chewing gum

Chewing 'chewing gum' has been popular in Britain since the end of World War II. This particular practice now has positive dental health benefits. Quite simply, the very act of chewing stimulates the flow of saliva which counteracts the effects of acid in the mouth. Some of the chewing gums once contained sugar which may in itself, as we have already explained, be part of the acid-producing process. But some chewing gums now contain sugar substitutes, thereby sidestepping this problem. Some flavoured gums freshen the breath and we are encouraged to believe that we are all the more kissable as a result!

Vegetarianism

Although we have included this section at the end of our discussion of diet, there is an increasing trend towards vegetarianism, and you should not feel that it takes second place in our consideration of nutrition. We have already discussed eating fibrous natural foods as opposed to manufactured foods so it seems reasonable to mention vegetarian eating at this point.

Some kinds of vegetarian diets do lack some of the B group vitamins and, if you are or wish to be a vegetarian, it is a good idea to discuss your diet with a doctor before embarking upon it. Certainly, chewing tough, fibrous foods stimulates the jaw muscles, the teeth, and the gums but you should not overindulge in this kind of chewing. In one instance, the author did examine a twenty-year-old woman who had complained of sensitivity in several of her teeth. The only explanation that seemed plausible was that the enamel of her teeth was very thin in the first place and that changing to a vegetarian diet had worn it away in several places over a number of years. Whatever you choose to eat, moderation is the best policy.

The value of bread

Bread contains little fat or sugar, and both brown and white bread provides about 15 per cent of the average daily requirement of energy in the form of starch, as well as protein, fibre, calcium, iron, thiamine, etc. Thus, it should be recommended as a useful part of the diet. Don't be tempted, though, to smear it liberally with jam or other confections but accompany it with vegetables, cheeses, and fruit.

EROSION OF THE TEETH ... A GROWING EPIDEMIC

We have already mentioned how drinking fizzy drinks containing sugars can lead to tooth decay but, since the previous edition of the book was published, there has been an ever-increasing problem concerning the enamel of many people's teeth. The problem is that a drink need not contain sugar to cause tooth decay. The drink may itself already be acidic and will break down tooth enamel just as if you dropped a piece of metal into an acid bath. Tooth enamel is very vulnerable to continual immersion in acid drinks. And, if you brush your teeth immediately after drinking these acidic drinks, you are simply compounding the problem because the enamel is **more** vulnerable at this time, as it has been weakened by the acid, and you are then assaulting it with the toothbrush.

Among the first characteristic signs of tooth-enamel erosion are:

1 some degree of sensitivity;
2 changes in the surface texture of a tooth;
3 as the enamel thins, the darker dentine beneath starts to show through and the teeth look darker;
4 the tips of the teeth can thin, split, and become jagged;
5 in some cases the restorations (fillings) which have been placed in or on teeth do not erode while the tooth substance around the fillings does so that the restorations look high and unsightly.

Once it has been damaged, tooth enamel cannot be replaced but it is possible to veneer the teeth to protect them and to reduce future damage. Your dentist is the best person to advise you.

1 Try to reduce the number of carbonated (fizzy) drinks that you drink.
2 Do not allow fizzy drinks to stay in contact with your teeth for long periods; drink them through a straw or swallow soon after imbibing.
3 Do not brush your teeth immediately after you have had an acid drink.
4 Chew gum as it stimulates the flow of saliva.
5 Do not avoid fruit juices; although they contain fruit acids they also contain valuable nutrients and vitamins.
6 As we have mentioned elsewhere, even stewed fruits are quite acidic. It is as well to be aware of this and perhaps a good idea to take a drink of water after a pudding or snack of this kind.
7 Read the labels on the bottles or cans to find out which chemicals the drinks contain;

In the first, 1986, edition of this book, Neil Curtis mentioned that all food products should be adequately labelled. The dental profession has always been wholeheartedly behind the idea of legislation of foodstuff labelling. Now that the problem of obesity has hit the headlines, it would seem to be the ideal time for carbonated drinks manufacturers to label their products properly.

③ TREATMENT

This book is essentially about preventive dentistry. Many people, however, never receive professional dental advice because they are put off by the thought of undergoing dental treatment. We have decided to describe some of the procedures that are carried out to treat dental disease in the hope that with this knowledge 'a visit to the dentist' will seem much less daunting. But there is another good reason for adopting a preventive approach – it is somewhat futile for any repair work to have to be repeated. But, once your mouth has been restored to sound health, you can then begin, with renewed vigour, to develop a high level of oral hygiene. Of course, after the treatment has finished, the well-contoured restorations (fillings and crowns) should make it much easier for you to clean your teeth and gums thoroughly.

THE DENTAL EXAMINATION

There are two sides to a first visit to a dentist – the patient's side and the dentist's side. (*See* Table 2) You should try to explain to your

Table 2 Dental jargon		
Surface of tooth	**Symbol**	**Location**
Buccal	B	Cheek side of upper and lower molar and premolar teeth
Lingual	L	Tongue side of lower teeth
Palatal	P	Palate side of upper teeth
Mesial	M	Surface of tooth closest to the middle of the face
Distal	D	Surface of tooth most distant from the middle of the face
Occlusal	O	Chewing surface of molar and premolar teeth – upper and lower
Incisal	I	Cutting edge of the incisor teeth, including the canine teeth – upper and lower

e.g. An MOD cavity is one that extends over three surfaces, the mesial, the occlusal, and the distal surfaces dentist, as clearly as you can, what, if anything, is troubling you at the time, and also provide a coherent summary of your dental history. If you are taking any medication that has been prescribed for you by a doctor or another dentist, it is a good idea to carry with you written details of the treatment. Strictly, it is illegal to treat children under the age of sixteen without the consent of the parents and, although consent is inferred if the child visits the surgery anyway, it is better for a parent to accompany him or her.

When you first visit a dental practice for an examination and/or treatment your dentist will probably begin by asking you a series of questions, or perhaps you will be asked to complete a fairly detailed questionnaire. Try not to be offended by this – your answers are very important and will be treated in the strictest confidence. For example, if you are a woman taking the contraceptive pill, it is essential that your dentist should know because some drugs that are used to treat dental infection may affect the potency of the pill.

You may be asked to provide the following information:

1 Name
2 Address
3 Age
4 Occupation
5 Date of last visit to a dentist
6 Medical history

(*This is an extremely important section and the reasons for asking such detailed questions are explained in Chapter 9.*)

Tick the conditions (if any) which apply to you.

☐ Have you at any time suffered from rheumatic fever?
☐ Heart disorder of any kind?
☐ Diabetes?
☐ Liver disease?
☐ Disease of the respiratory system, that is, the lung?
☐ Epilepsy?
☐ Have you undergone any surgery, such as removal of tonsils, in the past?
☐ Do you smoke? If so, how many? Cigarettes, cigars, pipe?
☐ Are you pregnant or a nursing mother?
☐ Do you take any medication regularly prescribed by your doctor or otherwise?
☐ Are you now or have you ever been addicted to drugs of any kind including alcohol?

☐ Have you taken any of the following drugs during the last two years? (*See* Chapter 9.)
    anticoagulants
    steroids (*See* Figure 18, p. 126, Steroid Warning Card.)
    tranquillizers
☐ Are you allergic to any drugs?
☐ Do you suffer from any other conditions that your dentist should know about?

7 Dental information

☐ Do your teeth or gums cause you pain?
☐ Do you suffer from pain in your jaw joints?
☐ To your knowledge, has any lump or swelling developed around your teeth or jaws?
☐ Have you ever had a tooth extracted?
☐ After a tooth has been extracted or after an injury, do you bleed excessively?
☐ Do any members of your family bleed excessively?
☐ Do your gums bleed when you brush your teeth and gums?
☐ When was the last time a dentist took radiographic pictures of your teeth?
☐ Do you like the appearance of your teeth?

X-ray examination

Radiographic examination involves the use of X-rays; in the doses used in most dental practices, X-rays are not harmful but, in any case, a strict safety code should be adhered to. In fact, since the first edition of this book was published, it is now general practice for dentists to have their radiographic equipment checked at least every three years by the National Radiological Monitoring Board using film monitors or through on-site inspections. The Health and Safety Executive continues to address this matter and your dentist may have a certificate of adequacy displayed at the practice. The main risk during a radiological examination is to the dentist and staff because they are in close proximity, so that proper guidelines and precautions are in everyone's interest.

Just after the second edition of this book was published, it was recommended that the use of protective lead aprons for patients prior to radiographic examination was not essential except when the X-ray beam was likely to pass through the trunk. Lead aprons are now actually contra-indicated when having the full mouth X-ray, known as an orthopantomograph, which shows the teeth and jaws in full (see page 161). Most dentists, however, avoid radiographic examination of pregnant women. If radiographic examination is required in a pregnant woman, the middle trimester is considered to be the safest period.

Radiographic examination of the teeth and jaws provides a wealth of valuable information. The dentist can determine whether the teeth have become decalcified which, in turn, suggests that tooth decay is present, how deep the decay has penetrated, and how close to the pulp it has reached. The radiographs will also reveal the presence of unerupted teeth in the jaw bones and the angle at which the third molars or 'wisdom teeth' might be lying. Fragmented roots of teeth, too, might be shown up indicating previous attempts to extract teeth. In addition, the presence of extra supernumerary or supplemental teeth might be demonstrated.

Sometimes, teeth may be congenitally absent and this will be established by radiographic examination. It is also valuable for the dentist to ascertain in this way the number, length, and configuration of the roots before any treatment on the pulps of the teeth is carried out. The dentist can check for any fractures of the jaw bone which may have occurred after an accident or injury, and any fractures of the teeth will be revealed too. The pictures will highlight any bone reabsorption which may have taken place as a result of periodontal disease, and the presence or absence of any cysts or tumours in the jaws will be established by this kind of examination.

Radiographic dental examination has a variety of other uses. For example, it has been used on the remains of Egyptian mummies to determine the state of the dentition, and it is sometimes the only method that can be used to identify the remains of bodies that have been burned beyond recognition after an accident. Indeed, forensic odontology, as it is called, is a fascinating subject.

Additional checks

Once the teeth have been thoroughly examined, it is important to check for any disease in the gums and surrounding structures. As we have explained in the previous chapter, periodontal disease leads to the formation of pockets between the gums and teeth. If the depth of these pockets is greater than 2 millimetres, it suggests that the disease is progressing uncontrolled. The dentist can check for the presence and depth of pockets using a special blunt instrument, called a pocket-measuring probe, which is graduated in millimetres and which will slide painlessly between the gum and tooth.

Any lumps or areas of discoloration on the gums might suggest that an abscess is developing on the side of a tooth which is not causing any pain. If such an abscess opens up and bursts, a small tract, called a sinus, will form from the pocket or the root canal to the outer surfaces of the gum. This is a chronic infection and should be treated. Remember that it is not just conditions which hurt that may need to be treated, and any source of infection must be eliminated.

If you have had all your teeth extracted you should still be vigilant about the health of your mouth. We do recommend that anyone, including especially the older man or woman, who wears full dentures should visit the dentist every six months. Elderly people occasionally suffer from vitamin deficiencies and iron deficiency anaemia; these conditions can easily be detected by a dental surgeon from the colour of the tongue and other tissues in the mouth. This would also tend to bring dentists into a closer association with the aged in the community. But young denture wearers can also benefit from regular dental examinations because the mouth often mirrors the signs of other diseases. It is important to investigate the causes of mouth ulcers or any other lumps that 'don't go away'. If you wear dentures and you are aware of soreness in the corners of your mouth, it may mean that your dentures are worn down and should be replaced.

TREATING TOOTH DECAY

Sometimes, you may find that your dentist does not treat tooth decay at all. In a child's mouth, for example, it may be kinder and more beneficial simply to ensure freedom from pain and to see that the contact areas between the teeth are self-cleansing. Quite often this results in hardening of the dental tissue in the region so that restoration of the teeth is unnecessary. In some cases, painting the surface of the cavities with fluoride actually encourages hardening of the enamel and dentine.

To treat tooth decay, the dentist will begin by injecting a local anaesthetic solution (see Chapter 8 for further details of controlling the pain associated with some kinds of dental treatment) so that the area becomes numb. The undermined tooth enamel and decayed or carious dentine can then be painlessly removed with a dentist's drill. Even when the undermined enamel and dentine have been removed, residual decay can still lodge in the tooth and this must be excavated using various instruments. Then the floors of the cavity are probed to make sure that they are hard and healthy. Tooth cavities are named according to their position on the tooth as shown in Table 2.

If the decay has destroyed wide areas of the tooth, the dentist can fit tiny screws or pins into the dentine which will support the filling material. To make this procedure easier and more effective, a stainless steel band is placed around the tooth; it can be tightened or loosened as necessary to contour it to the healthy tooth margins. Ideally, the dentist will position small wedges between the band and the adjacent teeth so that self-cleansing areas and surfaces that are easy to clean are provided.

Dental amalgam

Generally, the cavities are filled with a silvery coloured material called dental amalgam. Essentially, this is a mixture of silver, tin, and mercury, with small amounts of copper added to increase its hardness. At first, the amalgam is soft and is placed into the tooth from a special packing gun. Finally, the dentist packs the amalgam tightly against the walls of the tooth cavity. Dental amalgam is an excellent filling agent because it is durable and because it expands and contracts at the same rate as the surrounding tooth material in response to changes in temperature. It is long-lasting so that fillings rarely have to be replaced – an advantage because each time a tooth is filled the surrounding tooth is weakened slightly.

Mercury is a poisonous metal, of course and, in 1994, reports in the media caused some alarm among the general public concerning the safety of amalgam fillings. Dental amalgam has been in regular use for at least 100 years and so far, despite extensive worldwide research, no link has been established between the use of dental amalgam and any disease in humans. In fact, people who eat fish as a regular part of their diet are taking in just as much mercury from the fish as from fillings and, in parts of the world such as Iceland where a lot of fish is eaten, average mercury levels in humans are ten times higher than they are in Britain. Even though filling material should always be mixed in special machines in a well-ventilated area, dentists and their staff could be exposed to higher levels of mercury vapour than most people but, once again, research into their health has established no link whatsoever between the use of amalgam and any physical or mental disease. In conclusion, the Department of Health's Committee on Toxicity's stated view is that dental amalgam is not harmful to health. Of course, though, the best policy is to ensure that your teeth and gums stay healthy so that you do not have to have fillings of any kind.

Fillings in front teeth

Nowadays, these types of filling materials are tooth coloured and are readily available. Originally, white filling materials were a mixture of a form of silica and a mild acid which, when set, was quite resistant to the action of fluids in the mouth. Unfortunately, this material tended to shrink so that, after a while, the filling would fail. It also discoloured. Although, for many years, the material was the best available and the acids used were mild, they were inclined to cause some damage to the tooth's pulp, sometimes after many years. Nowadays, a hard, white 'quartz' type of material is used which, while it owes its origins to the original silica compounds, it does not have their disadvantages and keeps its colour-matching properties more effectively although some shrinkage still occurs.

Acid etching

Like the fissure sealants that were mentioned in Chapter 2, another new technique has now been developed whereby the white filling material can be bonded to teeth. Firstly, the tooth is etched with a mild acid and then the white filling material is bonded to the tooth. There are no injections, no drilling ... good news! Thus, an important new dimension, known as adhesive dentistry, has been added to dental treatment. Using this technique, not only simple and more complex cavities can be restored but the whole face and shape of a tooth can be enhanced. The latter technique is known as veneering and is dealt with in Chapter 7 on oral and cosmetic surgery.

Gold fillings and crowns

Fillings can also be provided in gold, although cost is a limiting factor. In this case an impression is taken of the prepared cavity and a dental technician casts a model from the impression. The model of the cavity is filled with wax and carved to the required shape. The wax pattern is then invested in plaster and, when this has set hard, the wax is boiled out and gold, at very high temperature so that it is liquid, is spun by a casting machine into the hollow in the plaster. The result is a precision casting in gold of the wax pattern which can then be cemented into the tooth. If a large area of a tooth is destroyed by decay, or fractured, or if the tooth is simply unsightly, the whole crown of the tooth can be rebuilt and its appearance will be considerably enhanced. It is not only the film stars of Hollywood who can benefit from cosmetic dentistry.

A cap or crown completely replaces the diseased or discoloured enamel of a tooth but the tooth must be prepared to receive it. Having given the patient a local anaesthetic, the dentist prepares the tooth (see Photos 1 and 2). The thickness of the shoulder around the preparation depends upon the type of crown that is to be fitted and, in Photo 1, we have shown the design for a full porcelain jacket crown. Normally, an impression of the tooth is then made. After root

1 A porcelain jacket crown about   2 A porcelain crown fitted to an
to be fitted to an upper left central   upper left central incisor.
incisor.

canal treatment has been carried out (*see* Figure 15, page 67), a metal
post is inserted into the canal of the tooth and the overall impression
taken. When the impression is removed from the patient's mouth,
the post comes away with it. From this the dental technician can cast
a gold or precious metal post which will fit snugly into the canal. This
can then be covered with a porcelain jacket crown. Using this procedure where a post is fitted may be referred to as a 'screw-in' type of
crown. It is not that the crown is screwed into the bone but that a
post is made to fit into the root canal and this is designed to support
the artificial crown. (*See* Photo 3.)

A gold crown can be provided on any tooth from the most obtrusive one at the front to the most hidden back molar. It is a matter of
taste. Clinically, however, if the bite is particularly heavy in the molar
region, a gold crown may be recommended. (*See* Photos 4 and 5.) It
is slightly softer than enamel, however, so that a gold crown is less
likely to harm opposing teeth. Porcelain, on the other hand, is harder
than enamel and may wear away some of the enamel on an opposing
tooth. In thin sections, gold is stronger than porcelain, too, so that, in
preparing the tooth for a full gold crown, less of the tooth substance
needs to be removed. In a porcelain-to-gold bonded tooth, enough of
the tooth has to be removed to allow for the thickness of the two
materials. Upper molar teeth, which often show when we grin, can be
faced with porcelain while the biting surface remains in gold. The
colour of the porcelain can, of course, be matched very closely with
that of the tooth enamel.

3 A 'screw-in' type of post crown about to be fitted to an upper right lateral incisor. Note that the post goes into the root and not into the gum.

4 (*below left*) A gold crown about to be fitted on to an upper left first molar.

5 (*below*) A gold crown fitted on to an upper left first molar.

Bridgework

In Chapter 1 we explained why missing teeth need to be replaced. Bridgework restores appearance and function after teeth have been lost and, provided the supporting structures of the teeth are healthy, it is often more desirable to have fixed bridgework rather than a removable denture. For bridgework, a tooth is prepared as if a crown was to be fitted and then the crown is joined to an adjacent tooth so that only the space from which the tooth is missing is restored. Thus,

6 Bridgework to replace an upper right first premolar. Note the prepared supporting teeth of abutments.

7 The bridge has been fitted to occupy the space of the original dentition with no plates. Note that the middle unit rests just over the gum. This area must be cleaned by dental floss and/or the use of an irrigation device.

there is no 'plate' in the mouth which can press on the gum and perhaps cause damage. The supporting crowns are cemented to the teeth so that the appliance need not nor, indeed, can it be removed easily from the mouth. Effectively, it mimics the original dentition and should last for many years. No one need know that you have had bridgework in your mouth and you will avoid the embarrassment that dentures cause among some people. (*See* Photos 6 and 7 above.)

ROOT CANAL TREATMENT

If the decay has reached the pulp of the tooth, it will be painful, sensitive to hot and cold drinks or food, and tender to the touch. The tooth can still be saved by root canal therapy (endodontics). When decay has reached this sorry state, the nerve and blood vessels can be in varying stages of disintegration but, to simplify matters, we shall assume that the decay has only just reached the pulp as shown in Figure 15.

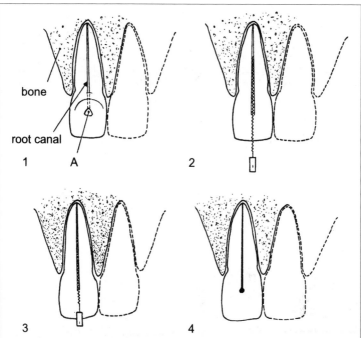

Fig. 15 Root canal treatment. Note that the process is much more complicated for molar teeth with three canals and can be quite time-consuming, including several visits to the surgery, if the canals are infected.

1   Hole made in the back of the tooth at A to give access to the pulp in the root canal.

2   Barbed broach used to remove the pulp.

3   Files and reamers used to clean canal. Spiral filler used to spin paste into canal. Gutta percha placed in canals to obtain good apical seal.

4   Gutta percha filling in root canal. Hole in palatal surface filled with amalgam or composite. If the tooth becomes discoloured a post crown can be made. (See photo 3.)

In this case, a radiographic picture of the tooth is taken to reveal how many root canals there are and how long they are. Then, the tooth is locally anaesthetized and access to the canals which contain the nerves is achieved. Next, a fine piece of barbed metal is inserted into the canal to a predetermined length to remove the infected nerve and the canal is dried with paper points. The canal is dressed with an antiseptic solution on a fine paper point and sealed in place with a dressing. If the tooth remains trouble free for a period of about seven days, then a permanent filling can safely be inserted into the canal. There are many of these available, ranging from strips of silver to plastic points. Finally, a permanent filling, inlay, or crown can be placed over the 'root-filled tooth'. Even if the whole of the tooth has been destroyed and the canal has been filled, it is still possible to construct a post crown to restore the tooth.

Recently a new device for measuring the length of a root canal has been developed. It is called an apex locator and, as the instrument being used by the dentist approaches the apex of the tooth, the machine makes a bleeping noise to indicate the nearness of the apex. This warns the dentist that he or she is reaching the final stages of cleaning and filling the root canal. The introduction of this kind of technology into dentistry is most welcome and very exciting, and it is very reassuring for the patient. It speeds up the process and increases the likelihood of complete success.

Abscess

If infected pulp is not treated, the bacteria in the root canal may set up an infection at the tooth's root apex, as shown in Figure 16. This is often extremely painful and requires urgent treatment. In some cases, the infection will spread to involve the glands in the face or neck and there is gross swelling. One way of dealing with this situation is to give the patient a general anaesthetic (*see* Chapter 8) and extract the infected tooth. In this situation it is not always a good idea to use a local anaesthetic because the needle may pass through infected tissue and spread the infection into healthy areas.

In some cases, say, for a front tooth of a young person, the dentist will try to save the tooth. Then the canals can be opened up, as we have described earlier, and, sometimes, some of the pus will drain away through the open tooth. If the tooth is treated in this way, the patient will need to be prescribed an antibiotic, such as penicillin, because the infection can continue to spread despite the open canal. If, following this treatment, the area of infection does not diminish in size, the gum over the root can be incised and the bone underlying it removed to expose the apex of the root. This can be cut away and the

infected apex

A

bone

B

C

D

1 before treatment   2 after treatment

Fig. 16 Chronic infection at the apex of a tooth which has not responded to root canal therapy may require apicectomy, that is, the removal of the apex of the tooth's root.
A Incision line. Gum reflected back. Bone removed. Apex exposed and severed.
B This area infills with bone.
C Cut end of root sealed with amalgam. 'Retrograde amalgam'.
D Root-filled canal.

infected area cleaned with a small, scoop-like instrument. Then the exposed canal is filled with amalgam (*see* Fig. 16) at the root end, the canal is reamed and cleaned from the crown end of the tooth, and finally it is sealed by an ordinary filling. This procedure to remove the apex of a tooth is known as an apicectomy.

TREATING GUM DISEASE

If you want to keep your dentition healthy, it is helpful to understand something about the condition of the gum and bone, or *periodontium*, which supports it. This understanding is one of the most important tools in discovering the factors which cause the disease and how it can be prevented. We cannot repeat too often that long-standing gum diseases (chronic periodontitis and chronic gingivitis) are the main causes of failure in restorative dentistry. Neither advanced crown and bridge work, nor even simple fillings should ever be provided if the patient suffers from uncontrolled plaque or gum disease. As one dentist summed up the situation, 'It is like putting new windows into a house while it is still burning down!' And, do bear in mind that certain systemic diseases of the body, particularly blood disorders, may increase the susceptibility to gum disease as we have mentioned in more detail in Chapter 9.

It is possible to establish whether or not the patient is suffering from gum disease by making several measurements. The plaque index is a measure of the amount of plaque which is present and is determined by using disclosing solution or tablets. We have already explained how the depths of the pockets between gum and tooth are measured – this is known as the pocket index. If the gums bleed severely, this can be estimated, too, to give a bleeding index. Finally, the amount of bone that has been lost as a result of a given disease can be measured to give a bone index. All of these factors are normally taken into consideration to give an overall picture of the progression of the condition. In fact, periodontal disease is very difficult to measure because it can involve only a few teeth and yet be very severe or involve the whole dentition and still be quite mild.

Among people after the ages of four to five years, gingivitis is extremely common. Indeed, research has shown that 90 per cent of the population of Britain suffers from the disease and, in one study on individuals between the ages of seventeen and twenty-two, all of those examined had periodontal disease. In children under the age of fourteen, it seems that there is more periodontal disease among girls than boys. (This may be associated with hormonal changes which occur at puberty making the gums more susceptible to irritation by plaque.) Similarly, hormonal changes which occur during pregnancy also tend to make the gums more susceptible to the disease. After the age of fourteen, however, boys become more likely to contract the disease because, as the textbooks suggest, it would appear that men and boys are less scrupulous in their oral hygiene. On the other hand, after puberty the prevalence of gum disease as well as its severity decrease until the young adult stage is reached when it increases again. Consequently, it is a great pity that the NHS in the UK has introduced charges for anyone over the age of eighteen because this is bound to discourage young people from seeking dental advice. At least the current capitation schemes do address this problem by allowing patients to budget for dental care and, at the same time, dentists are encouraged to provide as much preventive treatment as possible.

Today, the treatment of periodontal disease is being centred more and more upon instructing patients in sound oral hygiene measures, and dentists are assisted in this by well-trained dental hygienists. After the initial examination by the dentist, a series of appointments with the hygienist is arranged to measure the extent of gum disease and to eliminate areas of stagnation where plaque can readily accumulate. The patient's teeth are thoroughly scaled and polished and, most importantly, he or she is instructed and shown how to maintain a healthy dentition. In this part of the book, we are concerned with the 'surgical' approach to treating gum disease but, in Chapter 2, we have explained how mechanical and chemical aids can be used to keep the mouth healthy. Dental surgery should only be resorted to when other methods have not cured the condition completely in conscientious patients.

If the contour of the gums has been altered by the progression of periodontal disease and the condition has not been improved even by good oral hygiene, the gums can be recontoured surgically. This can either be carried out to a limited extent under local anaesthetic or there can be a full mouth recontouring under a general anaesthetic. The purpose of this procedure is to recontour the gums so that all the surfaces can be more easily cleaned. Unfortunately, it is possible that this technique may result in the exposure of the roots so that the teeth appear longer. Recontouring the gum (gingiva) is known as gingivoplasty and is carried out using a high-speed diamond burr in a dental drill or by electrosurgery whereby the gum is cut and the exposed blood vessels heat-sealed at the same time. This treatment is not quite as unpleasant as it sounds but it is still a better bet to control the plaque.

Scaling and polishing

Scaling the teeth thoroughly is perhaps the most important task that can be carried out for you by a dentist or hygienist but it is tiring for dentist and patient alike. The ultrasonic scaler has taken much of the hard work out of the procedure, however. This instrument, which is water cooled because of the heat that is generated, uses a curved probe vibrating thousands of times per second to produce a resonance that separates the calculus from the teeth. The principle is similar to that which is used to break up large stones that form in the kidneys.

After the teeth have been scaled, they are polished to remove any residual staining. Polishing with fine abrasive strips will also eliminate faulty ledges, known as overhangs, on fillings which would otherwise be plaque traps. In the case of heavy smokers where tar has coated the tooth itself, scaling may be needed to remove stains but the teeth must still be polished afterwards. Smokers who resort to tooth powders to remove staining should use them with care because they are very abrasive and, if you need to use them more than once a week, you would do better to give up smoking – for the sake of your general health if not for your teeth!

Evidence does suggest that smoking affects the gums. One particular investigation resulted in the belief that the chemicals in cigarette smoke actually reduced the number and efficiency of the body's white blood cells which are normally active in combating infection.

Chemicals in cigarette smoke may bind with red blood cell pigment at the site where oxygen would normally bind. It is generally believed that our red blood cells increase in number to keep the level of oxygen high enough to nourish the body. The body's reaction is therefore to produce more red cells. This has the effect of thickening the blood so that more work is required by the heart muscle to pump blood around the body. This is a strain in itself but, in addition, nicotine also causes the arteries to constrict. The tiny blood vessels in the gum may become blocked and fluid will build up in these parts creating a larger number of areas where infection may become more likely. It is also proven that the flow of blood across the placenta is reduced in women who smoke during their pregnancy.

Do remember that even the very best-designed dentures are a source of irritation to the gum so, if you wear them, you should continue to be scrupulous in your oral hygiene. This is also true in the case of any appliances that are used to straighten the teeth in orthodontic treatment.

The gum and bone are also irritated by the stress resulting from uneven contact due to malocclusion, high spots on fillings, or the different wear patterns of the dental materials, such as porcelain, amalgam, gold, silicates, composites, and acrylic plastics, that are used. All of these may contribute to the strain which can be transmitted to the periodontium via the teeth. Given the same levels of plaque, the extent of gum disease will be increased in a dentition which has been subjected to more mechanical stress.

Where periodontal disease has involved expanses of bone around the teeth, pockets in the bone can develop. This condition must also be corrected surgically. Careful surgery, again carried out under a local anaesthetic, may arrest the progress of the disease. Generally, the bone does not grow again, though the tooth may tighten in the socket. Existing infection can be eliminated by surgery along with the pocket in which plaque could otherwise accumulate.

Gum recession

Some exposure of roots of the teeth occurs naturally as the teeth wear down and overerupt to expose the roots. The teeth become sensitive but there are various toothpastes available which may help to relieve the discomfort. It is a good idea to smear a small amount of one of these pastes on to the teeth so that there is a reservoir of paste on the gum where it meets the tooth. Do ask your dentist first to recommend a particular product to you. This is best carried out last thing at night because the flow of saliva is reduced during the night and the chemicals in the paste have longer to work on the exposed root surface. Even in a young, healthy, plaque-free mouth the gums may recede, however. The canine teeth are surrounded by large buttresses of bone which stand proud of the bone surrounding the other teeth in the jaws. As the toothbrush sweeps across the jaw, more pressure may be put on this bone than on any other part of the jaw bone so that the gum recedes and the underlying bone is resorbed to expose the root of the tooth. Using a medium or soft brush, rather than a hard one, may be helpful in reducing the problem.

It is possible that lasers may be used in the treatment of sensitive teeth. It has been claimed that a laser beam will seal the tiny tubules in the dentine when they become exposed and so reduce the sensitivity. There is more information on the use of lasers in dentistry in Chapter 11.

4. RESTORATION OF THE DENTITION – DENTURES

Did you know that:
George Washington, the first President of the United States, wore wooden teeth?
In times past, teeth were extracted from corpses on battlefields to be used in dentures?
The biggest producer of false teeth is the tiny European principality of Liechtenstein?

In the UK alone, more than eighteen million people wear a denture of some kind, and about two million of these people are under the age of thirty-five. Although it is hard to believe, until recently it was fashionable in some parts of Britain for fathers to arrange for their daughters to have all their teeth extracted and dentures fitted before they were married. The practice was not designed to prevent the daughter from biting her new husband but to save him money and the daughter toothache! Presumably, the thinking was that natural teeth are a nuisance and could be regarded as being expendable. Fortunately today, however, our knowledge is improving and more and more people are keeping a good number of their teeth for longer so that most dentures fitted are the partial ones which replace a few missing teeth rather than a full denture to replace the complete dentition. This does suggest that the preventive dentistry approach is having some effect which is encouraging because, although modern dentures may be cosmetically quite pleasing and comfortable, they are certainly no substitute for the natural teeth. None-the-less, one-third of the population of Britain wears dentures, and even people who wear full sets need to look after their mouths, so we have decided to include a chapter on the making, fitting, and care of dentures.

HOW DENTURES ARE MADE
Essentially, there are four stages in providing dentures: the impression stage; the bite stage; the try-in stage; and the fitting stage.

The impression stage
After the dentist has examined your gums and jaws thoroughly a impression of your mouth is taken. Impression material which, incidentally, is derived from seaweed, is made up from a powder mixed

with water until it takes on a jelly-like consistency. It is then placed in one of a number of standard trays which should conform roughly to the size of your dental arches. If the dentist should then find that there are any discrepancies in the finished impression, he or she may suggest that you return for another one to be taken after the dental technician has made special, close-fitting trays which should fit your mouth more accurately. Indeed, trays of this kind are usually required for partial dentures. Some patients do find one particular difficulty in having an impression taken. Sometimes, the impression material may irritate the soft palate and the back of the tongue which might cause the patient to retch violently. Usually, this problem can be overcome if the patient is advised to relax and breath slowly and deeply through the nose so that, effectively, the back of the throat is sealed as the tongue rises against the soft palate and the vomiting reflex is controlled. In the most extreme cases, however, the dentist may decide to anaesthetize the back of the patient's mouth using an anaesthetic spray.

When the impressions have been taken, they are wrapped in wet tissues and dispatched to a dental technician who pours plaster into the moulds. When the plaster has hardened, the cast is removed from the moulds and covered with a sheet of reddish-pink wax from which a wax rim is built up along the dental ridges. These are than returned to the dentist for the bite stage.

The bite stage

This is a vital part of the work and several important measurements must be recorded at this stage. Firstly, the wax blocks are trimmed so that they conform as closely as possible to the dental arch. The distance between the patient's nose and chin is measured with a gauge and the height of the wax is adjusted so that the jaws meet comfortably. The measurement can be based on an existing denture but must account for any wear that will have occurred in the old denture.

Remember that the denture not only replaces the teeth that have been lost but bone as well so that the thickness of the wax in all dimensions is very important because it may often be necessary to plump out the lips or cheeks if there has been much shrinkage or bone reabsorption. The lip lines, too, are drawn on the wax block so that the amount of tooth to be shown can be determined and then the centre line of your dentures is also recorded. In consultation with your dentist, now is the time to choose the colour, size, shape, and character of your dentures but you should try to be quite sure of what you want at this stage because, if you want them altered again, it will delay the final fitting of your denture. You may be tempted to match new dentures with your old ones or even look at old photographs of yourself when you had your natural teeth. But take care because dentures should enhance your appearance. They should be cosmetically pleasing and unobtrusive, and it may be that flashing white pearls showing no signs of wear will not suit your face. After all, it really is not a compliment if a child says to you, 'My goodness, what lovely false teeth you have grandma!'

The try-in stage

By the try-in stage, the technician will have set up the denture according to the dentist's measurements and your personal taste. At this point, any minor alterations to the bite can be made and the appearance of the dentures can be changed if you wish, provided that chewing efficiency is not ignored at the expense of appearance.

The fitting stage

Assuming that all the previous work has been carried out satisfactorily, the fitting stage should be the simplest of all. The dentist will position the dentures in your mouth and check the bite and the appearance. There are various factors, including muscle control, which influence how snugly the denture will fit in your mouth. You will find that the action of your tongue as well as the movements of your lower lip will give some support to the denture as does the upper lip which binds against it. If you have just had old, worn-out dentures replaced, you will probably find that the new ones will feel very large, and any increase in the thickness of the plastic wall will restrict your tongue space a little, as well as altering your speech slightly. Don't worry. This should not last long and may not even occur at all but, even with the best-fitting dentures, they may need easing at the fitting stage or later on if they begin to feel tight. After a new denture has been fitted, some patients find that they gain extra confidence by using a denture fixative to hold the new set firmly in place. Many proprietary products are widely available from chemists and you should not feel that you have failed if you use a fixative for the first few days. It should not normally be necessary to use a fixative all the time but your dentist will tell you if it is advisable.

After you have had a denture fitted, you should not feel that you have to live on a diet of soup and soft foods for ever, but it will take a few days, or possibly weeks, before you will be able to master eating hard foods. Dentures will improve your appearance, help with your speech, and make it easier to eat, so it is small wonder that sometimes they do not always match up to the patient's expectations.

Sometimes the dentist may fit an immediate denture as soon as any teeth have been removed. These should not be taken out for at least twenty-four hours after the natural teeth have been extracted because they function as a pack for the bleeding tooth sockets. Initially, therefore, this type of denture should be worn at night. Permanent dentures can also be worn while you are asleep but it is better to remove them because they are 'foreign' to your mouth and the gum tissues do need time to relax. After a few months, immediate dentures may need to be relined because the bone has filled up the sockets from which the teeth have been extracted or has shrunk in other places. This is to be expected and you should return to your dentist to have another impression taken using the denture itself as the impression tray. From this the technician will add more of the plastic material to the fitting surface to improve the fit.

CLEANING DENTURES

Like your natural dentition, dentures must be kept scrupulously clean. It is a good idea to do this over a plastic bowl filled with water because it is all too easy to drop them on to a porcelain sink or basin when they might be damaged or broken completely. Once again, there are a great many denture cleaning aids available from chemists but it is still worth asking your dentist to advise you. Don't be tempted, though, to use household bleach to clean them, even if they are badly stained, because bleaches will irritate your mouth and craze the plastic of the denture. If they are so stubbornly stained that you cannot clean them with the normal preparations, go back to your dentist; usually, for a minimal charge, he or she will arrange for them to be thoroughly cleaned by the dental technician who will obviously use the correct technique and polishing equipment.

Even if you do break your dentures they can usually be repaired quite quickly – certainly within twenty-four hours. If the work is carried out under the NHS in the UK, it is free of charge at the present but, if the dentist you approach did not fit them, if you require an express service, or if the technician charges more than the standard NHS fee, the dentist may decide that a small charge is required so it is best to ask first. Because more and more dentists are finding it difficult to provide laboratory-based work within the budgets allowed by the National Health Service, capitation schemes, such as those provided by Denplan, do help to address this problem. Within the monthly premium, the dentist's costs and time are covered so that the laboratory charge can then be paid directly by the patient, helping to take the sting out of paying.

CORRECTING DISCOMFORT

From time to time, you may find that your dentures feel very uncomfortable. If you think that this has been caused because the design of the denture has mechanically irritated your mouth, it is a good idea to continue wearing the dentures for a few hours before consulting your dentist. This may sound harsh because it will make your mouth sore but, from this, the dentist can easily and accurately locate the site and cause of the problem. It is not just the design of the denture itself which affects how well it fits. If your mouth becomes particularly dry as a result of a decrease in the production of saliva, which may in turn be caused by illness or some forms of medication (*see* Chapter 9), the denture may become loose. Under normal circumstances, there is a thin film of saliva between the denture and the gum so that the surface tension actually helps to hold the denture in position, rather like the way a thin film of water will hold two flat sheets of glass tightly together. Sometimes, if the mouth is particularly tender, the only solution to the problems of irritation may be to place soft lining in the dentures but, as a rule, these do absorb moisture and are less hygienic than the harder plastic material from which the denture is made.

In some patients, the bony ridges may have shrunken so badly that there is little tissue left to support the dentures, or they may be so irregular that it is inadvisable to fit a denture. In these cases, the problem can be corrected quite easily by minor surgery, often in hospital, to deepen the sulcus and smooth out the ridges. Bearing in mind the huge number of dentures that are provided, there seem to be very few people who need this kind of treatment. If the dentures are very unstable an advanced procedure can be used to implant metal pins into the jaws on which the dentures can rest. (See page 100 – implants.)

OVERDENTURES

Once again, the most positive approach is to try to conserve the teeth whenever you can. Even though the crown of the tooth has to be lost, it may be possible to save the root. The root can be treated as described in Chapter 3 and then a small stud type of attachment is placed on to the root so that it can be received by the denture to help with stability. The canine teeth, especially, have very large roots which can accommodate these studs quite readily. This kind of denture is referred to as an overdenture (*see* Figure 17) and, if the teeth are not diseased, they are kept clean, and there is no gum disease, untreated teeth can be covered in this way to enhance the appearance without the need for extractions. It is particularly valuable for teeth that have become discoloured or badly worn down and,

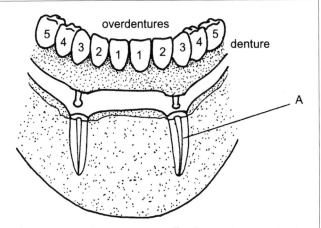

Fig. 17 Overdentures. Note that the cuffs of natural gum around the canine roots must be kept as plaque free as possible.
A   Root-filled teeth (canines) with stud attachment which engages a component in the fitting surface of the denture like a stud fastener.

because the roots remain in place, there is little or no shrinkage of the bone so that this type of denture is preferable. Of course, the supporting teeth roots need to be cleaned very carefully to prevent plaque from accumulating around them. Remember that, just like a dental bridge, the success of a denture depends upon the structures which support it.

The table on the next page shows the advantages and disadvantages of three commonly used dental materials.

PARTIAL DENTURES

As shown in the table on page 80, partial dentures, which only replace a few missing teeth, can be made from various materials. Whatever material is used, however, good plaque control is essential to the health of the mouth because plaque will attach to the denture itself as well as lodging between gum, tooth, and dentures. Partial dentures constructed from chrome cobalt material have a number of advantages. Unlike plastic, which is not strong enough to be used in thin strips, partial dentures made from chrome cobalt need not cover the roof of the mouth (*see* Photos 8, 9, 10 and 11). Therefore, although the majority of the taste buds in the mouth are in the tongue, there are a few in the palate and these are left free with

Table 3 Denture materials comparison table

Acrylic plastic	Chrome cobalt	Gold
Cheap to make and a cheap material.	Expensive to make but cheap material.	Expensive to make and very costly raw material.
Weak material – needs to be used in large amounts and cover all the palate.	Very strong material – can be used in fine section. Palate can remain free.	As chrome.
Repairs inexpensive.	Repairs more difficult and more costly.	As chrome.

Advantages and disadvantages of commonly used dental materials.

8 A model of a partly edentulous upper jaw.

9 Dentition of the upper jaw restored with a chrome cobalt denture. Note that it is resting on natural tooth and gum and that the palate area is free from pressure.

chrome cobalt dentures so that eating is more pleasurable. The chrome material is also conductive while plastic has an insulating effect, so that the comforting feeling of taking a warm drink is not impaired by a chrome cobalt denture. Dentures of this kind stain less readily, too, and are easier to clean but, as you might expect, they are more expensive to make than their plastic counterparts.

10 A model of a partly edentulous lower jaw.

11 Dentition of the lower jaw restored with a chrome cobalt denture.

Gold may sometimes be used in the construction of dentures, particularly if accuracy in casting is important but there is little or no clinical advantage and gold dentures will obviously be costly. Nowadays dentures can be made in virtually unbreakable material although this, too, is expensive. In case of emergencies, some patients ask their dentist to supply them with a spare set. There is no provision for this under the UK National Health Service and it would seem to be something of a luxury which should not be provided by the welfare state.

Occasionally, it may be difficult to make a partial denture stable in the mouth so that they are made with clasps which fit around the teeth. Patients do complain that these clasps erode the tooth enamel but, if they have been correctly designed, this will not occur and, in nearly every case, it is inadequate plaque control around the clasp which has resulted in tooth decay. Sometimes the clasps are designed so that they rest on as well as around the teeth. This tends to distribute the pressure of the bite to the existing natural teeth as well as to the gum and bone below the denture, so that the denture is said to be 'tooth and tissue borne'. This design is to be recommended because dentures which are tissue borne alone invariably cause undue pressure on the gums resulting in the 'gum stripper' denture.

Very rarely small infants may require dentures because some or all of their teeth are congenitally absent. Anodontia, as it is called, is very alarming for parents who may be comforted to some extent by the knowledge that dentures can be made and that children tolerate them extremely well. Children's dentures must, of course, be replaced very frequently as the child grows. Remember that anodontia may be associated with other illnesses which should be treated by a medical practitioner.

ALLERGY TO DENTURE MATERIALS

Allergy to denture material has been well documented but, fortunately, it is very rare. If you think that you may have such an allergy, do mention this to your dentist before the denture is made. Then, in conjunction with dental consultants at a hospital, a patch test can be carried out with the assistance of a skin specialist. Samples of denture plastic are applied to your arm and, if a weal develops, it shows that you are allergic to this material. It is unlikely, however, that you are allergic to all denture materials and a compromise can usually be reached.

REGULAR CHECK-UPS

It has been suggested that full denture wearers should only need to visit their dentist about every five years. We are convinced that this is by no means satisfactory because it assumes that visiting the dentist is concerned only with teeth. But, as we have already explained, the mouth mirrors the health of the whole body, and aged people, who are more likely to be wearing full dentures, may suffer undetected vitamin deficiency. This can quickly be diagnosed by the dentist who can then recommend the correct treatment for the patient. Older people are often lonely, too, and welcome the chance to talk to someone, so that their dentist and doctor can be very helpful in this respect. In addition, dentures may wear down and cause soreness at the angles of the mouth – this can be corrected by adjustment. More rarely, it is possible that a tumour can begin in or around the jaws which, because it may be painless, would otherwise remain undetected. If the tumour should be malignant, regular visits to the dentist and prompt treatment may even save life.

As we have explained, the trend today is towards keeping more of our teeth for longer so that full dentures are becoming less necessary than partial ones, but it would still be better if people did not require dentures at all. In any case, we should try to develop the idea that a dentist examines the mouth, jaws, and teeth, rather than just the teeth, and treats the patient rather than just the dentition.

5 THE WISDOM TEETH AND EMERGENCY ADVICE

Thankfully, we have come a long way from the time when the tooth drawer would set up his stall in the market place, painfully to remove teeth from the weary poor, which would then be set in dentures for the not-so-weary rich. Despite the progress we have made, however, stories still abound that, 'He had to put his knee on my chest to get the last one out, it bled for weeks, and I'm still not sure he took the right one out anyway!' Don't be put off. Most people like to embellish the facts, especially when it involves the dentist, and tales such as these simply cannot be true today. In the first place, if a tooth does not yield to moderate force (and it was once said that women could not make dentists because they are not strong enough!), then the dentist will take a different approach, perhaps involving minor surgery. Secondly, not even the most robust individual could survive bleeding profusely for more than a few hours without suffering a profound drop in blood pressure. And lastly, although it may be possible for a dentist to extract the wrong tooth, such cases are rare in the extreme.

We continue to stress that you should try to retain your natural teeth and that the best way of doing so is to maintain a strict regime of oral hygiene and visit your dentist regularly. Still, teeth must sometimes be extracted for a variety of reasons:

1 A tooth is causing pain and, despite any proposals for treatment by the dentist, the patient insists that the tooth should be extracted.
2 A tooth may not perform any useful function in the mouth and simply becomes a plaque trap.
3 The tooth has overerupted to such an extent that it fouls the bite and has become hopelessly loose because of its migration out of the supporting bone.
4 The teeth in the jaws are crowded and space must be made so that the teeth can be rearranged orthodontically (*see* Chapter 7).
5 A tooth has become so loose due to gum disease that it is uncomfortable, and any efforts to stabilize it would be unsuccessful.
6 A tooth is buried in the jaw bone and is unlikely to erupt without causing extreme discomfort or will be functionless when it does erupt, for example, an unerupted wisdom tooth in a full denture wearer. (*See* photo 12.)

12 A radiograph of a nineteen-year-old female. Note the partially erupted third molar pressing against the second molar.

7 Radiotherapy to treat tumours around the jaws will affect the capacity of the bone to heal so that it may be advisable to extract any suspect teeth before the therapy to avoid any healing problems later.

8 Teeth may be fractured at or below root level in, say, a fight or a road accident. If the fracture is vertical, then it is probably best to remove the tooth. Similarly, if the jaws are fractured, any teeth in the line of the fracture are usually extracted because they may provide a pathway for infection to the healing fracture site.

9 Anyone who is embarking upon a long expedition to a remote part of the world may decide that it is prudent to have suspect or, say, unerupted wisdom teeth extracted to avoid problems or pain while they are away.

10 The patient may decide that there are cosmetic or cultural reasons to have a tooth extracted.

METHODS OF EXTRACTION

It may not always be necessary but, before your dentist extracts a tooth, it may be wise for a radiographic picture of the tooth to be taken to show the angle of the root or roots and the density of bone around the tooth. The picture may also indicate if the tooth has more than the usual quota of roots.

Firstly, of course, the area from which the tooth is to be removed is anaesthetized (*see* Chapter 8), so having a tooth extracted should not be a painful procedure these days. Then the dentist will use forceps to remove the tooth. There is a variety of types of forceps but they are all designed to grip the root of the tooth, rather than the crown, so there is no need to think you are in for a major ordeal because your tooth is badly decayed or broken down to gum level. In every case, the tips of the forceps are inserted so that their arms press down in the lower jaw or up in the upper jaw, between the bone and the tooth, to sever the attachment of the root to the surrounding bone via the periodontal ligament. At the same time, this also has the effect of expanding the bony socket so that the tooth should yield with only moderate pressure. When the tooth has been removed, the dentist will normally place a gauze pack over the site to reduce the bleeding. It is possible that, after you have left the surgery, this may become dislodged but it is not difficult to replace it yourself and we have included a diagram to help. Almost certainly, your dentist will explain to you any post-operative care that may be required following an extraction. (*See* Figure 21.)

WISDOM TEETH

The third molars, or 'wisdom teeth', which erupt after about the eighteenth birthday may cause special problems by becoming 'impacted'. In simple terms, an impacted tooth is one which has not erupted and is either partially or completely embedded in the jaw bone. Usually, it is the impacted lower third molars which are the source of most of the exaggerated stories.

This seems an appropriate point for Neil Curtis to add a personal anecdote to help allay the fears of anyone about to have a wisdom tooth extracted.

In my case, the tooth was impacted and the dentist recommended extraction in hospital, perhaps under general anaesthetic. The hospital in question, however, preferred to carry out the operation under local anaesthetic because the extraction looked reasonably straightforward and there seemed little point in unnecessarily taking up a hospital bed. I sat in the chair white-knuckled and perspiring freely from a childhood fear of extractions. First came the topical anaesthetic and then the local by syringe – a good start, it was virtually painless. After a short while the dentist approached and said, 'You'll feel some downward pressure.' I did, and then braced myself for the anticipated pain of extraction. The dental surgeon had by this time walked away from the chair again. I asked 'When are you going to remove the tooth?' He smiled and showed it to me! I hadn't felt a thing and he had even inserted a soluble suture (stitch) to help prevent bleeding. Despite the nurse's advice to take paracetamol when the anaesthetic wore off, I had no need to for there was only a little soreness. There was virtually no post-operative bleeding and no swelling. The only disappointment was that I had nothing to show friends and family to demonstrate my fortitude at such an ordeal!

The third molars become impacted simply because there is not enough space in the jaw bones to allow them to erupt. This is partly because there is an evolutionary trend in humans towards a smaller jaw, but also, perhaps, because we eat less tough foods than our prehistoric ancestors, the apes, which might stimulate growth. If you compare the diagrams of the skull of a chimpanzee and of a human shown in Figure 18 you can clearly see that the chimpanzee's jaw bone is longer than ours so that there is more space for the third molar. The lack of space in the human jaw is worsened because the angle of the upright part of the jaw is more acute than in the chimpanzees. Incorrect suckling as an infant probably has an effect, too,

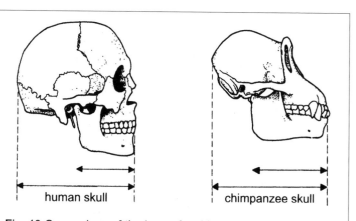

human skull   chimpanzee skull

Fig. 18 Comparison of the jaws of a chimpanzee and a human to show the space available for the third molar ('wisdom') teeth. The chimpanzee's jaw is longer in relation to its width than is that of the human. The angulation of the ascending part of the mandible is more acute in the human. This may be the reason why there is so often not enough space for the third molars. Other factors are involved but there may be an evolutionary change taking place which is resulting in a smaller jaw in the human while the number and size of teeth remain the same.

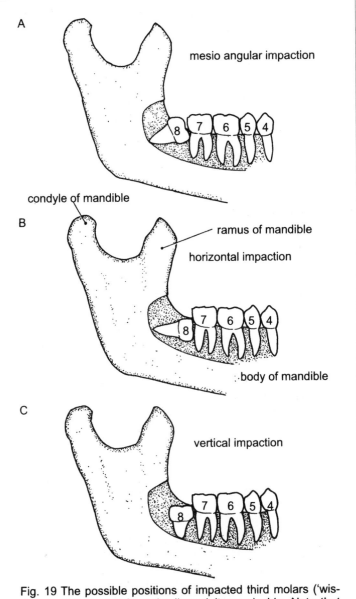

Fig. 19 The possible positions of impacted third molars ('wisdom teeth') viewed from the lingual (tongue) side. Note that nerves and blood vessels can be very close to the root tips of the third molars.

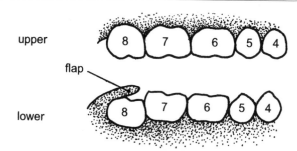

upper

flap

lower

Fig. 20 The 'gum sandwich' effect – not very tasty! The flap of gum over the lower third molar (8) is constantly bitten by the opposing third molar. Plaque can also lodge under the flap with the result that an infection is set up around the crown of the lower third molar – this condition is known as pericoronitis. This can happen during the eruption of any tooth, including those of the first dentition. (*Note* Upper 8 has fully erupted. Lower 8 is impacted against 7.)

as we have already explained. Any or all of these factors may be involved but impacted teeth may just be the result of genetic bad luck! From the diagrams in Figure 19 you can see some of the various types of impaction that can occur.

Treating impacted wisdom teeth, like treating any other type of crowding in the mouth, is an orthodontic problem (*see* Chapter 7) concerned with the spacing and arrangement of the teeth in the dental arches. As a wisdom tooth erupts, a flap of gum arises over its surface and, if the opposing wisdom tooth has already erupted and bites against this flap of gum, it will be very painful. One way of treating this is to remove the opposing tooth which is causing the trauma or, at least, to smooth its surface so that it does not bite the flap of gum. The erupting tooth then emerges uneventfully. Of course, if the erupting tooth is unlikely to come through in a satisfactory position, then it is best to extract the opposing tooth anyway because it will be functionless. (*See* Figure 20.)

The areas around erupting wisdom teeth are not easy to clean and many problems associated with wisdom teeth are caused by faulty oral hygiene. Any plaque which remains around the erupting tooth can cause the gum to swell painfully. Indeed, it is possible that many problems with wisdom teeth are entirely the result of incorrect oral hygiene and you should not assume that because you are the appropriate age and you are feeling pain from the corners of your mouth, that you will have to suffer the discomfort of tooth extraction.

Waiting lists for the surgical extraction of wisdom teeth are quite long but your dentist may be able to help you solve the problem simply with advice on dental hygiene.

There are advantages and risks associated with the extraction of problem wisdom teeth and you should discuss the situation with your dentist. The roots of wisdom teeth are close to the nerves and blood vessels which supply the lower jaw. If this is the case, your dentist should mention it to you before any operation is carried out because it may not be possible to avoid disturbing the nerves or even severing them during the extraction. Considering the number of difficult extractions that are carried out, there is only a very small percentage where problems persist but, if the nerves are severed, there is little chance of them rejoining and your lip and tongue may be permanently numbed on one side. If the nerve is only disturbed, rather than severed completely you will probably feel something like 'pins and needles' and, although it may take many weeks for the normal feeling to return, no permanent damage will have been done.

After you have had a wisdom tooth removed, your dentist will advise you on post-operative care. For every extraction in every individual, the surgery will be different so that only your dental surgeon at the time is equipped to give you the best advice, but we do feel that there are some general points which are worth mentioning.

In all branches of medicine and dentistry, every effort is made to limit the use of drugs and, except for the cases mentioned in Chapter 9, antibiotics are rarely prescribed for routine extractions unless there is an obvious risk of infection. When wisdom teeth are extracted in hospital, however, it is a routine procedure to administer antibiotics to the patient before surgery. You must make sure, therefore, that you do not take any drugs in any form which have not been specifically prescribed for the operation. As we have mentioned before, taking old tablets or other medicines may be dangerous while, if you use only a few antibiotic tablets rather than a complete course, you may risk developing in your body antibiotic-resistant bacteria.

After the operation, you should go home and rest. The dental surgeon will probably give you a pack of gauze to bite on and you should keep it in place over the socket as shown in the diagram (Figure 21) for about thirty minutes. Do not actively rinse out your mouth for at least twenty-four hours because, if you do, you may well dislodge or damage the blood clot in the socket. On the other hand, you can take a lukewarm, non-alcoholic drink after about three hours. If you do dislodge the clot, a dry socket may result and this is extremely painful. This may occur no matter how much care you take. A dry socket may be treated by packing it with a ribbon gauze

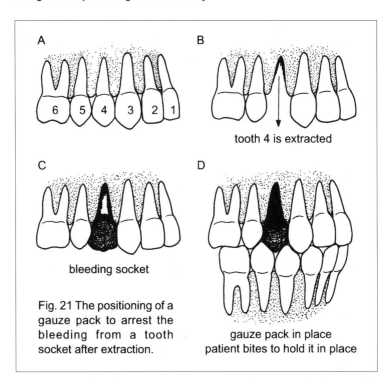

A

B

tooth 4 is extracted

C

D

bleeding socket

Fig. 21 The positioning of a gauze pack to arrest the bleeding from a tooth socket after extraction.

gauze pack in place
patient bites to hold it in place

soaked in a medicinal fluid, and with a prescription of antibiotics. The amount of pain suffered by each individual will vary and the dentist will prescribe pain killers according to need. If you find that pain persists for more than twenty-four hours, to the extent that it prevents you from sleeping, or it interferes with your daily routine, you should seek advice because the pain should not be that severe and may be due to an infection or to bleeding into the tissues. Remember, though, that you have had an operation and your mouth is quite likely to be sore for five days afterwards in the case of a routine extraction, or for as much as two weeks after surgery for an impacted wisdom tooth.

Swelling, known as oedema, is to be expected after surgery but it should not last for more than four days. Interestingly, lean elderly people seem to suffer from oedema less than younger patients. But, it is possible that bleeding into the tissues may occur so that a large blood clot develops resulting in the swelling of the area which becomes painful, and the muscles stiffen. This is treated with antibiotics and the use of hot, salt-water mouthwashes.

When you do rinse your mouth, use a solution of one table-spoonful of salt in a tumblerful of warm water. Avoid any other kinds of proprietary mouthwashes that have not been specifically prescribed because they may contain chemicals which will upset the clotting process. Make sure that the salt solution bathes the area as much as possible by keeping your head tilted on the side of the extraction as you rinse. If you are a smoker, avoid smoking for one week otherwise healing may be delayed and you may suffer from excessive pain. Don't be afraid to return to your dentist if any condition persists which worries you. Sometimes, you will find that your anxiety will be dispelled simply by the dentist explaining to you what is happening – reassurance is particularly important for children.

DENTAL EMERGENCIES

Bleeding tooth socket

If, after a tooth has been extracted, or for any other reason, bleeding cannot be controlled, this must be regarded as an emergency. Your dentist will probably have explained to you the action you should take but, in any case, you may find the following advice helpful:

1 A child or an adult should sit down and bite against a clean rolled-up handkerchief or gauze. The pressure of the swab alone may be enough to staunch the bleeding. (*See* Figure 21.)
2 If after fifteen minutes of this treatment the bleeding still continues, you should telephone your dentist, explain the problem, and arrange an immediate appointment. A child should always be accompanied by an adult. Even an adult should not go alone if he or she is distressed by a bleeding socket.
3 If the dental surgery is closed, then you should try to contact your dentist at home, assuming that he or she is not ex-directory or does not live so far away that it is impractical to see you late at night. In that case, you should get in touch with the casualty department of your local hospital and, nowadays, many counties in Britain run an emergency dental service to cope with just this kind of eventuality. The socket may require stitches (sutures) which does not mean that you have undergone major surgery because sutures are only intended to bring together the ends of a wound so that a healthy blood clot can be retained.
4 An emergency of this kind is best dealt with by a dentist but, as a last resort, you could seek the assistance of your general medical practitioner.

Emergencies in the surgery

It is possible that dental work, which would normally be completely safe when carried out on fit and healthy patients, can cause alarming and perhaps dangerous symptoms if the person is suffering from some ailment which is not obvious. Dentists are, of course, thoroughly trained to deal with emergency situations such as collapse or even respiratory or cardiac arrest. Obviously, it is much better to prevent such a situation and, if you are aware of any illness from which you are suffering or, if you take any kind of drugs, particularly ones such as steroids, anticoagulants, insulin, or antidepressants, you must inform your dentist. In any case, as we have explained in a previous chapter, you will be asked about your medical history on your first visit and it is vital, for your own sake, that you tell the complete truth. If a dentist is in any doubt, he or she will not proceed with the work until a full investigation has been carried out.

Pain is a warning sign and should not be ignored even by the most stoical individuals. Pain in a child may be difficult to track down and, again, you should waste no time in seeking expert attention. Swellings around the teeth, jaws, and face and neck region should also be investigated promptly. If your own dentist is unable to see and treat you on the day that you are suffering, then he or she might be able to arrange for you to see another dentist in the same practice or, indeed, somewhere else.

At weekends and during holiday time, emergency cover is provided in large conurbations. Many local newspapers publish the telephone numbers of duty pharmacists and emergency dental services and, at weekends and during Bank Holidays, local radio stations sometimes broadcast information about emergency dental services. In many counties, local hospitals also hold the telephone numbers of dentists who are involved in the emergency service. The newer organizations, such as Denplan, also provide a twenty-four-hour emergency service for registered patients.

In dental practice emergencies are:

1 Pain.
2 Bleeding from an area where a tooth has been extracted or injury to the mouth has occurred.
3 Acute swelling of the face and neck related to dental infection. This may be associated with an increase in body temperature.
4 Cosmetic problems. In this section, we include difficulties such as breaking your dentures or losing an artificial crown on a front tooth, for example. It is not always likely, however, that a dental mechanic will be available to repair a broken denture and denture

wearers should keep one of the denture repair kits to hand, especially during holiday times,
5 Accidental damage to the teeth.

Accidents to the teeth

When a tooth, especially a front one, is knocked out, accidentally or otherwise, then this is a genuine emergency. It is possible that, if you get to a dentist in time, say, within an hour, the tooth can be replaced in the socket successfully. Even if the tooth has fallen on to a dirty surface, such as a football pitch, pick it up and place it, if possible, either into milk or saliva. It has even been suggested that, provided there is no risk of inhaling or swallowing the tooth, you may put it into your mouth. This is not recommended for youngsters, however, nor for anyone who may have suffered from concussion. **Do not** store the tooth in tap water for the chemicals in the water may damage any soft tissues attached to the tooth. Nor should the tooth be kept in a dry environment. It is always worth making sure that your anti-tetanus immunizations are up to date and you should be able to tell your dentist if this is the case or not.

Contact your dentist and arrange for an appointment as soon as possible. Do not remove any strands of gum tissue from the exfoliated tooth. In the meantime, you should bite on a clean swab. When you go to the dentist, take the tooth with you for it may be that it can be replanted in the jaw. The tooth's nerve and blood vessels may already have decomposed by the time you get to the practice and the tooth may need to be root treated before it can be replanted. Don't be alarmed if the replanted tooth turns grey in colour – this is simply caused by the products of blood decomposition in the root canal. It can always be crowned later. Even first teeth can be replanted with the advantage that the spacing of the teeth is maintained. If a small child has a first tooth knocked out so that it literally hangs on a thread of gum tissue, you can place it back in the socket if you are sure there is no risk of the child inhaling the tooth. In fact, in many cases, first teeth retain the integrity of their nerve supply even after a severe trauma because the apices of the roots of these teeth are quite wide and reattach more readily.

A replanted tooth can be stabilized by splinting it to the teeth on either side with a plastic material. Even after just a few days the tooth may be quite firm in the socket. Replanting permanent teeth does not always work but there are many instances of exfoliated second teeth being replanted and remaining functional for years.

Some of the statistics associated with accidents to children's teeth are interesting and worth considering; and it is worth emphasizing again that gumshields should be provided when children participate in contact sports:

1 Even among children of pre-school age, boys suffer more injuries than girls. (Registrar General Reports, 960. Hardwick & Newman, 1954. J. Dent Research 33.730.)
2 It seems that children from broken homes are more accident prone than those from more stable backgrounds perhaps because any emotional disturbance caused by the break-up of a family may be manifested in violent physical behaviour in the child. (World Health Organisation, 1957. No. 118.)
3 Children with protruding teeth in both the first and second dentitions are more likely to injure these teeth than children with non-protruding teeth. In fact, in a survey carried out on a sample of 1,000 children, it was found that teeth are more likely to be damaged in children between the ages of eight and eleven years and that children with protruding teeth are five times more likely to fracture the front teeth than those with normal dentitions. (*See* Photos 20, 1 & 2.) (Hallett, E. M., 1953, Eur. Orth. Soc. 266.)
4 Observations of 118 children at the Turner Dental Hospital in Manchester showed that, among the younger children, trauma to the first teeth was more likely to occur between the ages of one and two years which seems to concur with the way in which toddlers normally behave. (Schreiber C. K., 1959, Br. Dent. J. 196.340.) The roots of teeth in the second dentition do not become mature until the younger person reaches the mid-teens so that, generally, permanent crowns are not provided for fractured incisor teeth in young people under the age of about sixteen. Temporary crowns may be made from white plastic material, however, but the tooth is not prepared so extensively as it would be for a conventional, permanent crown. Even if a crown is not fitted, the young person's appearance can still be enhanced using the acid etching techniques that we have described in Chapter 3.

After a blow to the face, your lips and cheeks may become very bruised and swollen so that your appearance is so distressing to you that you will seek treatment straight away. After a road traffic accident or a serious fall, for example, in which your face, teeth, or jaws have been injured, it is a wise precaution to have a thorough examination in the casualty department of a hospital. This should include a radiographic examination of the skull to check for any other fractures and, only after the doctors are completely satisfied that no other damage has been done, should you go to the dentist. Regard all injuries with suspicion until it is proven that all is well.

Swelling

An acute swelling or a high temperature may be associated with a dental infection and should be treated immediately. Any swelling in the body should be treated with suspicion and you should seek assistance straight away, but a swelling in the neck may be particularly dangerous because it can press against the airway as well as against the numerous blood vessels and nerves in this part of the body.

Dental infection

A dental infection can spread through the body very rapidly but, sometimes, the dentist can simply make a hole in the tooth so that the infective material actually drains away. This procedure will also relieve any pressure that has built up in the tooth as a result of the decomposition of the nerve and blood vessels and thereby relieve pain.

When infection enters the body, whether it is from bacterial or fungal organisms, or even by chemical means, the body's white blood cells are killed. Other chemicals, known as enzymes further break down the surrounding healthy tissue and the resulting creamy fluid is called pus. It is contained within a cavity to form an abscess. An abscess can burst spontaneously – you probably know what it is like to lance a boil. Incising is the clinical way of draining an abscess. The swelling caused by an abscess may not be painful and the most dependent part of it can be incised with a scalpel so that copious amounts of the foul-smelling pus are released. Minor surgery of this kind is not painful. The feeling of relief which comes when the abscess is incised is immense. To increase the body's resistance to the infective bacteria, the dentist may prescribe a course of antibiotics. Even if the infection responds very rapidly to this treatment, you should always complete the whole course of medication to prevent the bacteria from building up a resistance to the antibiotics. Only if there is an obvious allergic reaction to the antibiotic drug should you discontinue the course of treatment, and then you should return to your dentist to explain what has occurred.

An abscessed tooth is not always doomed to the surgery bucket, although it may be necessary to extract it when the swelling has subsided. It may be possible to treat the tooth and save it. Even if the infection stems from the gum rather than from the tooth itself, the tooth can still be retained. In this case, the area around the tooth would be thoroughly cleaned and scaled, and some periodontal surgery performed, but, again, the tooth may need to be root treated.

Treating yourself

We have already explained the treatment that is required to control the bleeding that may occur after a tooth has been extracted. If the bleeding continues you should only apply mechanical pressure to the socket and seek advice straight away. **There are no drugs used to control bleeding which you can safely administer yourself** and you should not, under any circumstances, attempt to do so.

When you have painful teeth and gums, well-meaning people often suggest remedies to relieve your suffering. This condition requires expert attention, however, and we must condemn the application of almost all kinds of unprescribed pain-relieving substances. Some people might suggest that you should place an aspirin next to the aching tooth but this can be most injurious because aspirin contains salicylic acid which will burn the gum tissue. You will be left with a raw, reddened wound with folds of dead, white skin at its edges – it will look rather like the affects of sunburn. Aspirin is a very effective painkiller, however, when taken by mouth as directed but it is an irritant to the stomach and, ideally, should be taken only after meals. Paracetamol, on the other hand, is far less irritating to the stomach but, if taken in large doses, it is likely to cause liver damage, which does not become apparent until some four to six days after the dose has been taken. Ideally, as we have stressed all along, all drugs should be taken only on prescription from dentally or medically qualified practitioners.

Even the tooth tinctures that can be bought from chemists can irritate the gums if they are used to excess. But, as we have stressed throughout this book, painful teeth and gums require the correct dental treatment and you should never use any pain-controlling medication for more than a few hours, especially in the case of children. It is no longer considered safe to give aspirin to children under twelve years and, even for older children, aspirin should not be administered without first seeking medical advice.

Antibiotics treat infection and are not pain controllers. Even if the pain is caused by an infection, you must not be tempted to take a small dose of old penicillin tablets that you may have lying about the house. This is only likely to increase the bacteria's resistance to the antibiotic and, anyway, you should not have any drugs left over from a previous treatment in the first place. As a general rule to be strictly observed, you should always dispose of any unfinished medicines safely and sensibly by returning them to a pharmacist or your doctor. Even if you do have drugs in the house which were originally prescribed to treat dental pain, never use them for different episodes of dental problems.

You may find it helpful to apply clove oil to a painful tooth but, once again, you should not be content with this treatment for more than a day. You must make an appointment to see your dentist. In fact, clove oil mixed with white zinc oxide powder is actually used by dentists as a temporary dressing. The dressing hardens, keeping the clove oil in contact with the raw dentine, and does help to minimize the pain from the tooth. It is really very effective!

Dental pain requires dental treatment and, unfortunately, we cannot recommend drinking whisky or any other alcoholic beverage to control pain, even though it was used as an anaesthetic in the past. Alcohol will raise the blood pressure and, if you have just had a tooth extracted, it may cause excessive bleeding from the socket.

There are now kits available (ask your dentist about them) which include such items as mirror, an applicator of dental cement, and temporary filling material to enable you to refix loosened crowns or insert temporary dressings into cavities your self – DIY dentistry. The kits also include a sterile needle which is vitally important if you are anywhere where you think a dentist might be reusing needles. The idea for these kits was developed in Britain.

We have already discussed the manufacture and fitting of dentures in a previous chapter but, if you do damage them, you should be able to find a dentist or a dental technician to carry out emergency repairs. It is even possible to buy products for denture repairs from some chemists and it is a good idea to include one of them in your emergency dental first aid kit which it is worth keeping in the house. Never use ordinary household adhesives to repair broken dentures for they often contain chemicals which, even after the glue had hardened, may irritate your mouth and damage your dentures.

Emergencies and the National Health Service

When the new National Health Service Contract came into force in 1990, dentists were required, as part of their care duties, to provide out-of-hours emergency treatment for registered patients. While many dentists already provided this service, its organization has been streamlined in such a way that large districts are catered for by fewer dentists who are 'on duty' on a rota basis. If you are abroad, however, or even a long way away from your usual surgery, you may have to pay more than you would normally for the service you are asking for. Again, the capitation schemes now available, such as the one provided by Denplan, cover emergencies of this kind through a rapid-response helpline and you can be put in touch with a dentist as close as possible to where you are. More recently, patients have been advised to contact NHS Direct.

⑥ COSMETIC DENTISTRY

COSMETIC DENTISTRY AND IMPLANTS

Cosmetic dentistry is perhaps one of the fastest-growing areas of dentistry and although, of course, most dentistry is to some extent cosmetic, there are some procedures that are carried out solely to improve the patient's appearance.

Veneers

The relatively new technique of placing facings on teeth to alter their shape and colour is the culmination of many years of research and development. Small gaps between the teeth can also be closed using this technique (*see* Photos 13 & 14). Put simply, the technique can be compared with placing a false finger nail over the existing nail giving an instant cosmetic improvement. In the mouth the facing, or veneer as it is called, must be: very strong; compatible with the mouth's soft tissues such as gum, tongue, and lips; easily cleansed; and, ideally, resistant to staining from food, drink, and tobacco.

The material that best satisfies these requirements is porcelain and dentists have been using this to make crowns for more than a century. When a crown is fitted to a tooth, a substantial part of the original tooth is necessarily lost but this does not happen when a veneer is placed. In some cases, the tooth remains largely, if not wholly, intact.

13 and 14 The gaps between the teeth were disguised and the smile was achieved using porcelain veneers
(Dr Surinder Hundle BDS, L.D.S.R.C.S. (Eng) C/o Lund Osler, Knightsbridge, London.

Dental implants

An implant is a metal screw inserted into the natural bone of the jaw under strict aseptic conditions in such a way that the head of the implant projects from the gum margin and can carry a supporting device for a denture or for bridgework. Dental implants probably involve more branches of science than any other surgical procedure in dentistry. The technique requires the skills and knowledge of dentists, dental technicians, oral surgeons, metallurgists, anatomists, physicists, and of course nurses. It is also very time-consuming. Thus, implants are very expensive and, only under exceptional circumstances, is this procedure available on the NHS. Similarly, some of the standard capitation schemes specifically rule out cover for either replacing old implants or placing new ones. There are, however, some dental finance companies that, subject to status, offer to finance particular dental procedures such as these.

The most important aspect of placing an implant is how long it will last. The whole implant procedure is designed to improve the lasting qualities of what is, in effect, a foreign body in the mouth without damage and without discomfort to the patient. It is also very important that patients to be fitted with implants are carefully chosen. Good oral hygiene is even more important for patients with implants than it is for people with normal dentition, for the site of the implant is a prime location for bacteria to lodge. Usually, the dentist will recommend that the patient should have a full medical assessment carried out by the patient's doctor. If, for example, the patient has any history of heart disease, he or she may not always be a suitable recipient for an implant.

There is a vast array of shapes and sizes of implants. One of the most successful materials used to make them is the durable metal titanium. One of the reasons titanium works so well is because, when it is exposed to air, it oxidizes. The oxide layer is very tough and resistant and causes no reactions in the tissues it is placed in, that is, it is inert. The latest implants are described as biocompatible, that is, the tissues of the body perceive them as a natural, compatible substance so that they are not rejected.

Usually, an implant can be placed under a local anaesthetic in the same way that a restorative procedure, such as a small filling, is carried out. Occasionally, the dental surgeon may suggest that, as well as the local anaesthetic, a sedative is administered too. Sometimes, the procedure takes place in hospital conditions and the patient is given a general anaesthetic.

In some cases, it may be quite some time after the implant has been placed successfully into the bone of the jaw that restoration of the dentition can begin. Bear in mind that the implant must be

15 A missing canine tooth in a young woman.

16 A metal implant is placed in the bone in the canine tooth space.

17 A porcelain crown is fitted over the implant to restore appearance.

18 As Photo 17 – front view.

19 Metal implants in upper and lower jaws.

20 The upper denture is fitted to metal implants. Fixed bridgework is seated on lower implants.

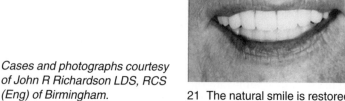

Cases and photographs courtesy of John R Richardson LDS, RCS (Eng) of Birmingham.

21 The natural smile is restored.

accepted by bone and by the so-called soft tissues. The bone must integrate with the implant, and the soft tissue – the gum – must adapt well to the oxide-coated metal collar which projects from the bone. To ensure that they are sterile, implants are stored in glass ampoules and are removed only as and when required. The dental surgeon will place the implant in such carefully controlled conditions that there is not even any risk of the talcum powder from his or her surgical gloves contaminating it. The implants are numbered so that their quality and the success of placement can be reported to the manufacturer.

Implants can be used to replace a single tooth or multiple units. They are also used to provide a supportive base for full dentures in those patients who have very small dental ridges. A small dental ridge, however, may indicate that the actual depth of bone is also limited so that, once again, suitable patients must be carefully selected.

BOTULINUM TOXIN (BOTOX), BLEACHING, AND OTHER COSMETIC PROCEDURES

Now, among the cosmetic procedures dentists already make available, many dental surgeons can provide their patients with anti-aging, anti-wrinkle techniques. The drug used is widely known as Botox. Used in very small doses, Botox paralyses muscle by interfering with the transmission of nerve impulses. In turn, this has the effect of relaxing those muscles that cause wrinkles and frown lines.

Botox came into its own as a treatment for eye squints (strabismus) and other nerve disorders but it had been used for at least twenty years to reduce wrinkles, and has become a very popular treatment for improving the appearance of the face. It is a tried and trusted therapy. Botox treatment usually lasts for about six months after which the nerve endings which have been blocked regenerate.

The drug bearing the brand name Botox is an extremely weak form of a toxin (poison) produced by the bacterium *Clostridium botulinum*, the same toxin which, in high doses, produces the dangerous, and sometimes fatal, food-poisoning illness known as botulism. While controversy still exists about the use of the botulinum toxin even in such a dilute form, the consensus of opinion appears to be that it can be used safely for such minor cosmetic procedures as those mentioned here. And additional uses for the treatment continue to be found. For example, it can be used to reduce sweating by injecting it under the arms and into the hands and feet.

Many people find that, if they look better, they feel better and, while celebrities may now admit to undergoing the procedure, it is no longer a treatment for the very rich and famous. It is relatively painless and the effect lasts for several months.

There is a school of thought that suggests that dentists are ideally suited to carrying out this procedure. Dentists are very familiar with administering injections around the mouth and they are given intensive training regarding the anatomy of the face, mouth, and lips. Recently, however, there has been a recommendation that anyone carrying out this procedure must be registered, and this is to be welcomed. It could be argued that, strictly, it is not dentistry although, in fact, restoring a patient's dentition also often has the effect of improving the appearance of the face. This effect may be further enhanced by the use of anti-wrinkle medication and the use of various fillers.

Are there any risks with Botox treatment?

Yes, there are.

1 It is possible that the treatment may result in eyelid or eyebrow droop which will take about three weeks to resolve itself. It has been argued, however, that this occurs only if the technique used is doubtful.

2 You **must** find out if you are allergic to human albumin before starting a course of Botox injections. You should **not** begin the course if you are.

3 Do **not** undergo Botox treatment if you are pregnant or breast-feeding.

Collagen implants

Another procedure that may be considered to lie within the remit of dentistry is the use of collagen implants into the lips. This technique enhances the fullness of the lips and, for those who find it appealing, gives an attractive pout.

Rehydration and rejuvenation procedures

Some dental practices and cosmetic surgery establishments offer procedures to rehydrate and rejuvenate the skin. Any patients who may be interested in these techniques would be wise to discuss them with their GPs as well as with their dentists. There is still debate about who should administer these kinds of treatments

Some dental surgeons are particularly interested in the procedures outlined above and, provided the practitioner has undergone the proper training and is fully insured, and provided the patient can feel assured of these matters, then it is up to the individual patient to decide whether or not he or she wishes to go ahead with the procedure. But don't forget, although the procedures do not involve surgery, the most stringent health and safety practices should still be applied, in particular, to avoid even the slightest risk of cross-infection

What should you ask?

1 Ask the practitioner to show you proof of attendance at the appropriate training courses as well as documentary evidence of his/her qualifications.
2 When, where, and how is the procedure to be performed?
3 What will be the full cost of the procedure? (Make sure that there are no hidden extras.)
4 Are there any finance plans available for this kind of treatment?
5 Will an anaesthetist be used? If so make sure that he/she is also properly and fully qualified.
6 If possible ask to see pre- and post-operative photographs of procedures that have been carried out by the practitioner who will be treating you.
7 How long does the treatment take and how long is it likely to last?
8 Ask for the exact names of any materials that are to be used in the procedure, including their product licence, and for how long they have actually been used in this treatment. Remember that some products are made from animal tissue while others are synthetic and it is the animal-based products that are most likely to cause allergic reactions.

BLEACHING

This is a cosmetic procedure that needs to be mentioned separately. It is a treatment for which there has been a huge demand. In Desmond Morris's famous book, *Manwatching*, first published in 1977, there is a photograph of an African tribeswoman in her ceremonial dress; her teeth have been filed to points and they are stained black. In her social circle this was considered highly attractive. There is a second picture in the book: this time it is of a European woman with full, bright-red lips and showing the most gleaming white teeth. Most people in most other cultures consider this to be attractive.

The two pictures lie at either end of the cultural spectrum but the concept that beauty is in the eye of the beholder is for ever true. Ultra-white teeth can look rather artificial but, in general, most people think that removing stains from the teeth and lightening their colour enhance their physical appearance. And it can be argued that, provided a person's dental health is satisfactory overall, then any procedure that brings someone into contact with a dentist must be a good thing. In some respects, physical appearance and wellbeing do go hand in hand.

Tooth bleaching can be carried out either at home or in the dental surgery. Each dentist has his or her own preferred method and, of course, the patient may decide which technique is most suitable.

Home bleaching

Do not buy home-bleaching kits over the counter or on the Internet unless you have first discussed the product and its method of use with your dentist. Go to you dentist and explain precisely what it is you want to do and to what extent you wish to lighten the colour of your teeth. You should also discuss with your dentist how much it is going to cost.

For the home-bleaching procedure, the dentist will make an impression of your upper and lower teeth using much the same kind of material that is used to take an impression for dentures. Taking the impression is quite painless. The impressions are sterilized and sent to a dental technician who then makes two casts so that he has exact replicas of your upper and lower teeth. Then the technician makes a thin Perspex tray which fits over the teeth leaving a reservoir space between the Perspex and the cast. In the same way, the tray can be fitted over your teeth leaving the reservoir space. You can then put the bleaching gel into the space using a specially designed syringe.

When you go back to your dentist, he/she will show you how to fit the trays into your mouth, how you should take care of them, and how they should be stored when not in use.

When you are at home, using the syringes, you fill the trays with the bleaching gel to about 30 per cent full. Remember, **do not over-fill** the trays: less is safer. Make sure that you wipe off any excess bleach from the trays before you put them in your mouth because the chemicals can be an irritant to the soft tissues. Place the trays over your teeth. You can leave them in place for a few hours while you are awake or put them in before you go to sleep and remove them when you wake up. Basically, the longer the bleach is in contact with your teeth the sooner you will get the results you want.

When you remove the trays, you should rinse out your mouth thoroughly and gently brush the gel off your teeth. It is then a good idea to brush them again using a fluoride toothpaste. Some patients complain of sensitivity after bleaching procedures, and the fluoride helps to lessen this effect.

You will need to wear the trays for several hours every day or night for at least three to five weeks to obtain the desired result. Most dentists will be able to show you tooth charts so that you can match the existing colour of your teeth and then decide the degree of whiteness that you would like to achieve. Many patients find that the procedure is perfectly comfortable and are satisfied with the end result. Remember, however, that your teeth are likely to darken again so that the procedure will have to be repeated. But, as your dentist has already spent time on providing you with instructions and has had the trays made, the 'top-up' treatment is, in most practices, considerably less expensive than the initial consultations.

In-surgery bleaching

In terms of the chemical that is used, in-surgery bleaching is not vastly different from home bleaching but the results are achieved much more quickly because the chemical's activity in the mouth is enhanced in the way described below.

Your dentist will give you a pair of protective goggles, rather like sunglasses, to put on. Your mouth is propped open and your lips are pulled back using special adaptors to expose your teeth. This doesn't sound very pleasant but it is not too uncomfortable for too long and it is important to protect your eyes and the soft tissues of your mouth from the chemical bleaching agent. Then a protective coating is placed over the gums and the bleaching gel is applied to the teeth. A powerful blue light is then shone on the teeth to activate the gel. In this way the bleaching effect is very rapid.

Because this procedure is surgery based and involves more sophisticated equipment you should expect to pay much more for it than you would for home bleaching.

Other methods of tooth whitening

Using bleaching agents on the teeth is not new but, in the past in the United Kingdom, the procedure most commonly known to most dentists was to use hydrogen peroxide on a cotton-wool pellet. Hydrogen peroxide has been used for decades to bleach the hair. Unfortunately, if a tooth had been root treated (*see* Chapter 3) sometimes it would darken instead of lighten. In that case, a small hole could be drilled into the back of the tooth into which the treated pellet could be sealed for a few weeks. In time, the hydrogen peroxide would whiten the tooth from the inside.

With tooth whitening now very much in vogue there is another chemical, not dissimilar to hydrogen peroxide, which can be used. It is called carbamide peroxide. The carbamide peroxide is in a glycerine base which makes it easier to apply.

Is tooth bleaching safe?

Do not proceed with tooth bleaching if you are pregnant or think you might be pregnant.

Do not proceed with tooth bleaching if you are breastfeeding.

Do not proceed with tooth bleaching if you have any mouth infection, tooth decay or gum disease.

Your dentist should ask you if you are pregnant or breastfeeding but we stress these matters here in case, despite our advice to the contrary, you are tempted to buy a bleaching kit over the counter or via the Internet without professional advice.

1 It is known that bleaching may cause sensitivity of the teeth but, so far as we are aware, this sensitivity is reversible, and no long-term discomfort has been reported.

2 If excess bleaching material is continually applied to the soft tissues of the mouth, the gums can become irritated and, rarely, ulcers may occur. Again, so far as we are aware, there have been no reports of any permanent effects.

3 *Does tooth bleaching alter the structure of the teeth?* It is now thought that bleaching does make the teeth temporarily more porous so one would assume that it must have some effect on the structure of the teeth even if any effect is only short term. Again, the porosity is reversible as the continued use of fluoride toothpaste and fluoride from the diet cause the enamel to re-mineralize to some extent.

4 *Does tooth bleaching affect the nerves and blood vessels inside the teeth?* The bleaching process is a chemical reaction and temporarily raises the temperature of the teeth. The nerve inside the tooth will respond adversely to greatly increased temperatures but we have not heard reports that any permanent pulp (nerve) damage has occurred from properly monitored, professionally applied bleaching.

5 Bleaching may affect the integrity of existing fillings (restorations). You should not bleach your teeth if resin-based, white fillings are to be placed within twenty-four hours. Of course, if you are undergoing tooth bleaching under professional supervision, then your dentist will guide you anyway.

6 The roots of the teeth may resorb even after the relatively innocuous procedure of internal bleaching but the effect is greatly enhanced when the light-activated in-surgery bleaching is used.

The latest thinking is that clinical studies are needed urgently to discover whether or not hydrogen peroxide-type agents cause tumours or if they cause any damage to the DNA of cells.

Furthermore, in all cases of in-surgery tooth bleaching the gums, and soft tissues generally, should be protected from the chemicals. Home-bleaching gels are considered to be safe at, but not exceeding, 10% concentration but all patients should be regularly and frequently monitored. Tooth bleaching should be avoided where there is tooth decay or where there is any disease of the mouth.

7 STRAIGHT SETS – ORTHODONTICS

Orthodontics is the name given to the branch of dentistry which deals with those conditions that result in a loss of chewing efficiency and/or the creation of an unacceptable appearance owing to the position of the teeth in the dental arches. Orthodontics is not an isolated speciality within dentistry but is an integral part of the whole subject. The need for orthodontic treatment is based on preventive, cosmetic, and functional considerations. The correction of a 'crowded dentition', for example, will facilitate adequate cleaning, particularly flossing.

According to a report published by the Welsh Office of the UK Department of Health and Social Security in 1973, more than 50 per cent of children have some kind of irregularity in their teeth. Of these, however, less than half need any kind of appliance (brace) to correct the problem – if it can be called a problem. We must stress that a deviation from what we might consider normal may not necessarily result in a loss of function nor the creation of an unacceptable appearance. Beauty is in the eye of the beholder!

The irregularities which can occur may interfere with the way the upper and lower teeth meet when the jaws are closed. A lack of contact in any region results therefore in a loss of chewing efficiency. The angulation of the teeth may lead to an unacceptable appearance, particularly in profile. Sometimes, these problems can be avoided by the well-timed extraction of some of the first teeth and, more commonly, the premolar teeth of the permanent dentition.

The pattern of meeting of the upper and lower teeth is referred to as the *occlusion* and, generally, the situation shown in Figure 3 (page 17) is the normal arrangement. Deviations from this 'norm' are referred to as *malocclusions*. The way in which the various malocclusions are classified enables dentists to communicate with one another more easily but, just for the record, the norm is referred to as a Class I occlusion, although individual tooth malpositioning can occur even in this arrangement.

Class II describes the situation in which the upper teeth protrude in the incisor region (*see* Figure 23). This condition can arise because of the undergrowth of the lower jaw, overgrowth of the upper jaw in the incisor region, or, in some cases, may also be caused by the habits of tongue thrusting, thumb sucking, or lip biting. Class III refers to

22 Orthodontic study models. *Top* Class II malocclusion before (*left*) and after (*right*) treatment. *Bottom* Class III malocclusion before (*left*) and after (*right*) treatment. (*Courtsey of Mr Richard Fieldhouse.*)

the condition which exists when the lower incisor teeth are in front of the upper incisor teeth when the jaws are closed. This condition is commonly associated with overgrowth of the lower jaw bone. (*See* Photo 22, lower models.)

Even though the improvement in appearance which can be achieved by orthodontic treatment is not the only factor which dictates the need for treatment, orthodontics is probably the first introduction that many of us experience to what is, in essence, cosmetic dentistry. Indeed, it is often the look of a child's teeth and jaws that prompts parents to seek advice.

Despite some reports, and even the comments that we have made in this book on the effects that modern diet and other environmental factors have on the teeth, most dental derangements have been shown to be of genetic origin. These genetic variations can, there-fore, result in disproportionate sizes of the teeth and jaws which lead to malocclusions and incorrect positioning of individual teeth. Though most dental irregularities of this kind are genetic in origin, we have also referred elsewhere to the possible effects of sucking habits on the dental arches. It is generally accepted that there is a connection between the development of the arches and the action of surrounding muscles which are those of the tongue and lips. The tongue is extremely strong and can exert considerable pressure on the front teeth – so much so that the teeth will eventually protrude. Placing the thumb in the mouth and sucking for long periods of time may further worsen an existing malocclusion. There is no direct evidence that tongue thrusting or thumb sucking actually cause a malocclusion but these habits almost certainly worsen a condition which already exists.

During a baby's first year, it may be that thumb sucking is due to dissatisfaction with breast feeding because the flow of milk to the baby is too fast but, more commonly, this is associated with bottle feeding. Decreasing the size of the hole in the teat of a bottle which is used to feed the baby will stimulate it to suck more. The instinct to suck in the newborn offspring of many species of mammals is particularly strong and we might even suggest that there is some sensory deprivation in babies who are not suckled correctly. We have already mentioned that preventive dentistry should begin at the ante-natal stage, and this is as necessary for orthodontic reasons as it is for the prevention of gum disease and tooth decay. You should be careful not to scold a child for thumb sucking; the best approach is gently to move his or her hand away from the mouth and to try to occupy the child's attention with other toys. In older children, hypnosis has been used to attempt to break the thumb-sucking habit. One report suggested that the children should be told that sucking the thumb alone was quite unfair, and that all the other fingers and the other thumb should receive equal attention. This would then become so tedious for the child that the habit is given up. If thumb sucking persists to an age at which the second dentition has erupted, the dentist can offer more practical help. Plates of different kinds can be fitted in the child's mouth but it is considered that this procedure is unacceptable for children under the age of five years.

An important factor in the development of malocclusions is the premature loss of some of the first teeth. Some parents assume that it is all right to lose some of the primary (milk) teeth because they feel these teeth are not important. This is quite wrong, however, and the first teeth are just as important as the permanent dentition. Premature loss of the first teeth can result in drifting and spacing of the other teeth which can lead to a malocclusion. Occasionally, when a tooth is lost, sadly through decay or accident, in a mouth where there is no other factor which could cause orthodontic problems, the dentist might suggest fitting a space maintainer. This is shown in Figure 22. It is only considered to be necessary if there is to be no extraction of permanent teeth for orthodontic reasons later.

Fig. 22 A space maintainer – often short term. This simple space-maintaining device is fitted around the tooth and is maintaining space in the 4-5 region (upper left).

The restoration of decayed milk teeth is also important in space maintenance, and the teeth may even tilt or drift into a space created by the loss of just a part of a tooth. Thus, it is extremely important to conserve the primary dentition. Good oral hygiene, and the application of the preventive techniques mentioned in Chapter 2 are also important for orthodontic reasons.

Orthodontic treatment is only recommended where the end result will give a lasting improvement. Sadly, in some cases, a relapse occurs after much effort has already been made. If the improvement in the dentition which has been brought about by orthodontic treatment does last, then the procedures have been justified.

An example of a common type of malocclusion is shown in Figure 23a (and *see* Photo 22). Occasionally, in this situation, the lower teeth actually bite into the palate at the back of the upper front teeth. The indentation formed by the tips of the lower teeth can ulcerate and become quite sore. The profile of a child with this problem is quite characteristic and his/her school mates may tease the youngster.

The condition may be treated by removing the sound premolar teeth as shown in Figure 23b and a brace is then fitted to retract the upper canine teeth into the space created. The other front teeth are then aligned in the arch by the labial bow (*see* Figures 23c & d). To balance the extractions, two lower teeth are often removed, too. Sometimes, molar 7 teeth, rather than premolars, are extracted, and the indications for extractions may also be based on the condition of the teeth. Usually, it is the first premolar teeth which are removed but if, for example, the second premolars were badly decayed or already had large restorations, then the dentist might be tempted to create space by extracting those teeth instead.

Where additional retraction pressure is required, appliances which fit around the child's head, may be used. These are called extra-oral traction appliances. Wearing such an appliance may cause

Fig. 23a A malocclusion class II, division I – prominent front teeth. Note that the molars and canines in the upper jaw are in advance of the lower molars and canines.

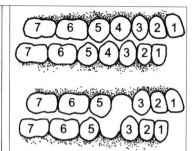

Fig. 23b The class II malocclusion in profile. The first premolars are extracted (upper and lower 4s). The right side is shown here but the left side is similar and all four teeth are extracted.

Fig. 23c An appliance is fitted to pull back the canine teeth, that is, the 3s are retracted using a canine retractor spring. A A labial bow is usually placed after the canines are back in the space occupied originally by the first premolars.

Fig. 23d An additional appliance then pulls back the four front teeth.

a sensitive child some embarrassment but it is hoped that the resulting improvement in appearance will be worth the upset.

The appliances shown in Figure 23c are referred to as removable appliances, and it is wise for children to take them out if they take part in contact sports or in swimming. Children, particularly, may benefit from the use of fixed, rather than removable, appliances to move teeth into the required position. Because the child cannot remove the appliance, he or she will be obliged to keep it in place even at school. These appliances can be very comfortable but, because they cover most of the teeth, they are hardly attractive to look at. It is to be hoped that if the child understands that submitting to this for a few months will eventually result in an improvement of the dentition later, the brace will not need to be worn against the child's will. Of course, good oral hygiene must be maintained throughout the course of treatment. You can buy special tooth-brushes for cleaning the teeth when appliances are present.

Adults, even in middle age, may also have orthodontic treatment, although it is generally accepted that teeth move more quickly through young bone. To speed up the movement of teeth through the bone in adults, it is possible to carry out an operation, known as *corticotomy*, in which, under a general anaesthetic, the bone around each tooth is cut away. Braces are then fitted to the teeth, as usual, but the end result is achieved more quickly. Operations of this kind are normally carried out in hospital by a consultant orthodontist and/or an oral surgeon. It must be borne in mind that some orthodontic procedures may take as long as two years to be completed, and even moving only one tooth may involve three months' treatment followed by a period of retention.

It is possible that a malocclusion may be due to a gross abnormality of the bony development of the jaw. Many people may be worried by the appearance of their teeth and jaws, and your dentist may not wish to draw your attention to the problem for fear of upsetting you. If you are in any away concerned about such a condition, therefore, do ask your dentist about it because it is likely that it can be corrected. For example, even an extremely prominent lower jaw, such as the one featured in Photo 22, can be corrected by orthodontic treatment. Of course, the improvement in appearance, following an operation of this kind, will be considerable. In fact, the condition shown in the illustration is known as Habsburg Jaw because it was a hereditary feature of that royal family.

Orthodontic treatment is a highly specialized and extremely important branch of dentistry and, with the improvement in oral hygiene so that we are better able to keep our teeth and gums healthy and free from decay and disease, it may become even more necessary and popular in the future. Remember that it may assist greatly in controlling plaque by reducing the crowding in the mouth and minimizing the areas of plaque stagnation. Bear in mind that orthodontic treatment should not be forced on children and that careful discussion with your child at home is extremely important. Indeed, it may well be worth making an initial visit to your dentist without your child to arm yourself with information that you can pass on to him or her.

The timing of orthodontic treatment is quite crucial, and a dentist will not want your child to wear an appliance for too long. Unless there is a fairly rapid initial improvement in the dentition, the child may well lose heart, and the removable type of appliance will spend more time on the child's desk at school than it does in the mouth. Fixed appliances do not have this disadvantage but, of course, they are usually only constructed where multiple, difficult tooth movements are to be carried out.

Your dentist may recommend that, even after treatment is complete, your child should continue to wear the appliance at night time only. Please make sure that you follow this advice to the letter. Relapse of orthodontic malocclusions, because the appliances were not retained long enough, is not uncommon. Orthodontic treatment using appliance therapy is normally begun in the child's eleventh or twelfth year but it is important to seek advice frequently before this age.

Clean the orthodontic appliance with a toothbrush and water. Instruct your child to fill a bowl of water and to clean the appliance over the bowl. If the child drops the appliance while cleaning it, then it will fall into the water and not break. In this way, valuable time and effort will not be wasted.

TOOTH ODDITIES

We have already mentioned in a previous chapter that some of the teeth may be partially absent. Sometimes, the spaces which result from this *partial anodontia* can create an unacceptable appearance or loss of function of the teeth. In some cases, this condition can be improved by the use of orthodontic appliances and partial dentures. In adults, sophisticated bridgework can be employed.

Some people have extra or *supplemental* teeth. These may cause crowding and may need to be extracted. Where there is extra dental tissue present in the mouth but it does not closely resemble the shape of the natural teeth, it is referred to as a *supernumerary* tooth. Such teeth do not always erupt fully and may impede the eruption of the natural teeth. A supernumerary tooth may appear in the midline, the so-called *mesiodens*. The supernumerary may not be causing pain but its presence may cause spacing between two front incisors, for example. Extraction of supernumerary teeth is not a major operation but it does generally involve an overnight stay in hospital because a general anaesthetic is invariably needed.

When some of the first teeth are retained in the lower jaw and the permanent successors have already erupted, parents often become quite alarmed about this situation. There is no need to worry. The retained deciduous teeth are simply removed and, in most cases, there is no lasting damage to the dentition (*see* Figure 24).

You will see that irregular tooth positions may be due to a variety of dental tissue abnormalities, and to undue pressure placed on the teeth by muscular activity, such as thumb sucking. A rare occurrence

Fig. 24 Retained deciduous teeth. These can be extracted and the central incisors behind them will move forward in most cases into a favourable position. This usually occurs in six- to eight-year-olds.

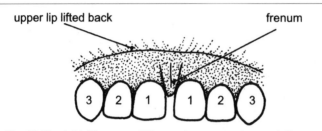

upper lip lifted back   frenum

Fig. 25 The labial frenum of fibrous tissue creating a midline space between the upper central incisors. The frenum can be removed surgically in a short operation, usually performed under a local anaesthetic only.

is the presence of an enlarged *frenum*. This is the band of muscle and fibrous tissue which extends from the inner surface of the upper and lower lips to the gum between the front incisors (*see* Figure 25). It may have an unacceptable appearance in itself but it also often maintains a space between two incisor teeth. This may be treated by reducing its size surgically under a local anaesthetic. If, however, there is spacing elsewhere in the dental arch, the space between the incisors may not close even if the frenum is reduced in size.

Where there is an obvious spacing present between teeth but there are no teeth missing, a radiographic examination may reveal cysts, tumours, or odontomes. Cysts are not uncommon in young people. Collections of cells, sometimes leftovers of development in the embryo, enlarge and absorb more fluid than the surrounding tissues giving rise to the formation of a cell-lined, fluid-filled cavity or cyst. To remove it, the patient may require a small operation under general anaesthesia.

Thankfully, tumours are quite rare but, obviously, they must not be overlooked and, once again, any dental abnormality should be investigated, even if only to eliminate this condition as a possibility.

Odontomes are bizarre collections of odd dental tissue. Sometimes, they are reminiscent of enamel, dentine, or cementum and sometimes mixtures of all these tissues. They are not dangerous but they may undergo cystic change to cause spacing of the teeth.

Gemination (twinning) may occur occasionally in the primary dentition, though not exclusively. In this condition, the crowns of the two teeth fuse together while they are forming and, although they occupy their usual position in the arch, they may appear to be slightly smaller than the total width they would have been, if they had appeared in the usual way. They rarely require removal and, indeed, it is merely worth bearing in mind that the demarcation line between the two crowns may be a plaque trap.

Replanting teeth that have been lost in an accident is intended to maintain the correct spacing, and the orthodontic aspect of replacing such *subluxed* teeth should not be ignored. Another orthodontic procedure which is not uncommon is replanting teeth which have become buried in the jaw. One good example of this condition may occur with the upper canines, as is shown in Figures 26a, b & c. The canine tooth can remain totally unerupted and not cause any pain or discomfort. When it becomes necessary to pull this tooth into the arch because of the possibility of it causing problems later, the dental surgeon may extract the first premolar tooth, extract the canine, and replant it in the prepared socket of the premolar. Sometimes only the crown of the canine tooth is exposed, in which case a splint cap is

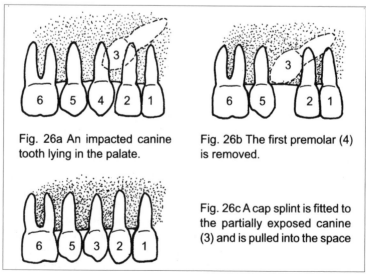

Fig. 26a An impacted canine tooth lying in the palate.

Fig. 26b The first premolar (4) is removed.

Fig. 26c A cap splint is fitted to the partially exposed canine (3) and is pulled into the space fixed to the crown, and, using another tooth as an anchorage point, a system of wiring is used to pull the canine into its proper space.

You will have realized that orthodontics is not a line of treatment to be entered into lightly and it is worth remembering the following points:

1 Timing of the treatment is important.
2 All other aspects of dental care are just as important in orthodontic treatment as wearing an appliance.
3 The method used to feed your baby may affect the alignment of the teeth – sucking habits can worsen the condition.
4 The treatment may involve the extraction of healthy teeth to lessen crowding.
5 The condition may only be improved and not necessarily cured.
6 Take care not to impose your will on your children.

Some orthodontists now provide removable appliances made from different coloured plastic materials – and some will even ask the dental technician to incorporate glitter into the material! This is intended to help the child tolerate the appliance, and even add a touch of humour. And, in a family with twins where both are suffering from the same orthodontic condition, differently coloured appliances can aid identification.

If children play contact sports, fixed orthodontic appliances can cause injury. Although it is difficult, it is possible to build mouth-guards that cover the teeth and the brackets of the fixed appliance. Sometimes, the orthodontist will provide an appliance that does not actually move teeth but harnesses the natural growth of the jaw and encourages its muscular development. These are called functional appliances.

NEW TECHNIQUES IN TOOTH REPOSITIONING

Patients and dentists have always been aware that wearing ortho-dontic appliances does pose some problems. Orthodontists and dental appliance companies have worked very hard to customize appliances and to make them more pleasing to look at. In the last few years, the metal brackets placed on teeth, affectionately known as 'train tracks', have been minimized, and the elastic bands which are used come in a wide variety of colours. And the fact that more and more children are benefiting from these treatments means that an individual child feels less self-conscious about wearing the appliance.

It is actually adults who are less enthusiastic about wearing 'train tracks'. It is this that has probably led to another development in orthodontic therapy, in which the brackets are fixed *behind* the patient's teeth. Where this is done, cleaning the teeth and gums must be thorough and scrupulous, and it may take time for the patient's tongue to become accustomed to the metal bits! Brackets placed behind the upper teeth are always more comfortable in this respect than lower-teeth brackets because the tongue rests mainly on the backs of the lower teeth.

Ingenuity among dentists is not a scarce commodity, and the latest orthodontic development has been the use of clear plastic trays that fit over the teeth. Each tray puts pressure on the teeth in the required directions. Because the trays are clear, they are less obtrusive and cosmetically more acceptable than the 'train tracks'. To make orthodontic trays, the dentist takes a model of the teeth and this is sent to a specialist company which then makes a series of models/trays and returns them to the dentist to be fitted at strategic times, thereby straightening the teeth.

This technique is acquiring some momentum in the United Kingdom. Of course, it would be up to the individual dentist to consider whether you should be seen by a registered specialist orthodontist to carry out this procedure.

⑧ ANAESTHETICS

ANAESTHESIA IN DENTISTRY

The story of how methods have been used to control pain spans many centuries and even the Greek poet, Homer, refers in the *Odyssey* to certain medicaments which affect sensation and feeling. The ancient Egyptians used Cannabis Indica as an anaesthetic, while the Greeks were familiar with the use of extracts from poppy plants, and the Romans developed mixtures of herbs and other plants that would cause a deep sleep. In some cases, the purpose was that patients should be unable to feel pain during surgical operations. Indeed, throughout history, many people have contributed to our current knowledge of anaesthesia.

In 1681, a book was published which drew attention to the use of gases as a means of anaesthetizing patients. On 10 December 1844, Gardner Q. Colton, a lecturer in surgery, spoke of the effects of nitrous oxide on the human body. One Samuel A. Cooley 'took the gas' and during the demonstration he bruised his legs and appeared to suffer no pain. This incident resulted in the dentist, Horace Wells, inviting Colton and another dentist, John Mankey Riggs, to perform a surgical extraction of a painful tooth. The patient was Wells himself. The tooth was extracted on 11 December 1844 and Wells, fully recovered, reported that he felt no pain, nor was he aware of the surgical procedure being carried out. On future occasions, Wells carried out this procedure in his own practice and the extraction of teeth under general anaesthetic was performed successfully on many patients. Wells was also familiar with the effects of the gas ether but he chose to use nitrous oxide. In 1845 Wells went to Boston, Massachusetts to bring nitrous oxide before the medical profession. He spoke to the class of John Collins Warren and tried to demonstrate the effects of nitrous oxide. In not giving his patient sufficient gas, or possibly by attempting to extract the tooth too soon into the anaesthetic, the patient reeled in agony and the entire audience hissed and jeered at Wells. He returned to his home town of Hertford, Connecticut deeply discouraged and dejected. Meanwhile, Wells's former partner in dental practice, William Morton had encountered much success using ether. In January 1847, Wells went to Paris and published a letter in the *Gallignani's Messenger* on 17 February 1847 claiming priority for the use of the anaesthetic, nitrous oxide. Ether, however, was recognized to be a superior anaesthetic agent, though Wells tried desperately to prove nitrous oxide to be so. Wells moved to New York and experimented on himself with other gases. On one occasion, on 21 January 1848, he became so deranged by the effects of some of these gases that he attacked a passer-by. He was arrested and imprisoned and, while there, on 24 January 1848, inflicted a wound on himself which severed an artery in his thigh and he bled to death. On 25 January 1848, these facts were unknown to the Paris Medical Society which, that very day, proclaimed Wells the discoverer of anaesthetic gases.

Anaesthesia had arrived and its advantages in surgery were recognized so that an eminent surgeon of the day, Mr Fergusson, reported in the second edition of his book, *Surgery*, 'It is, perhaps, not saying too much when this discovery is characterised as the greatest in most respects which has been made in the province of surgery'. Today, surgeons can painlessly transplant organs or carry out the most delicate operations without any discomfort to the patient.

Local anaesthesia renders only certain, localized parts of the body insensible to pain but it also has a long history. Most local anaesthetics used in dentistry are based on chemicals which are related to or associated with cocaine. Adrenaline is invariably added to the agent so that the blood vessels at the site of the injection constrict to keep the anaesthetic where it is meant to be. This also has the effect of reducing haemorrhage at the site of operation in case of surgery.

You will have gathered that there are two separate chemical ways of controlling pain during dental procedures:

1 General anaesthesia using the inhalation of gases, or the injection into the bloodstream of drugs which act on the brain and render the patient insensible to pain that way.
2 Local anaesthetics which act at the site of the surgery or which may be injected at some distance from the site to provide a regional anaesthetic or block.

It may be more straightforward to look at local anaesthesia first of all so that you will be able to appreciate why most of your mouth goes numb after you have had an injection for one filling in the lower jaw. (*See* Figure 27.) There is only one place where the main nerve trunk to the lower jaws and teeth is not surrounded by bone and this is at the corner of the mouth where the nerve leaves its main trunk and enters the canal in the lower jaw bone. An injection of a local anaesthetic solution here will anaesthetize the lip, tongue, and gum, as well

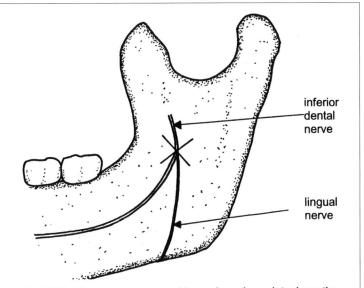

Fig. 27 The lower jaw, tongue side to show the point where the nerve enters the jaw bone. 'X' marks the spot where a local anaesthetic is inserted to make the tongue and lip numb. After this point the nerve to the teeth is within the jaw bone.

as the teeth, by a regional block. If a tooth is to be extracted from the lower jaw, the solution is also injected into the sulcus because there is another nerve supply here from a different source. Don't worry, then, if a good part of your mouth is affected after a couple of injections in the lower jaw – it is quite normal.

The upper teeth can also be anaesthetized by a regional block but it is more usual to use individual injections around each tooth that is to be treated or extracted. To make life even more comfortable the dentist can now use local, topical anaesthetic creams so that you will hardly feel the prick of the needle. It still hurts you more than it does the dentist, however! It is important to remember that some anaesthetic solutions may interact with other drugs if the patient is taking any so you must give your dentist a full and complete medical history, including any medication that you are taking at the time.

As the law stands at the present, a general anaesthetic can be administered by a dentist, although the General Dental Council advises that all general anaesthetics should be given by a trained operator other than the operating dentist. If the dentist who is operating on you also accepts responsibility for administering the general anaesthetic, then you could be placing yourself at considerable risk possibly with fatal consequences. It is not a good idea to try to serve two masters and it is well-nigh impossible for the dental surgeon to function as the operator and the anaesthetist without jeopardizing one of the tasks in the process. If you or your child has to have a general anaesthetic for a dental operation, then make sure that there is a properly qualified person present for each part of the procedure. If you are in any way unsure, don't let the dentist go ahead, for you could be putting you or your child's life at risk by your consent. Do not allow yourself to be the patient of an operator-anaesthetist.

Dental operations involving the use of general anaesthetics should be carried out by experienced and properly qualified anaesthetists who have access to the equipment that might be needed in the case of an emergency. It is permissible for a dentist to administer sedatives, such as diazepam (Valium), provided a second, suitably trained person is present. A simple sedation may be defined as 'a technique in which the use of a drug or drugs produces a state of depression of the central nervous system, enabling treatment to be carried out, but, during which, verbal contact with the patient is maintained throughout the period of sedation. The drugs and techniques used should carry a margin of safety wide enough to render unintended loss of consciousness unlikely.' In other words, a sedative is a drug which calms the patient, so that he or she is willing and able to undergo surgery, but retains enough faculties to speak coherently and respond to commands. Inhaling certain anaesthetic gases, such as those administered during the early stages of childbirth, may also be considered as drugs of sedation, as are those which are injected into the arm veins of a patient for the same purpose.

In all dental practices emergency resuscitation equipment should be readily available. Many dentists and staff attend seminars on resuscitation procedures so that all staff are kept up to date and patient welfare is never compromised.

Warning

Prior to a general anaesthetic patients should have been starved of all food and drink for at least four hours and, in some cases, dentists may recommend six hours. No tight or restrictive clothing should be worn. All previous medical history should be made available to the dentist and his or her anaesthetist, particularly liver, heart, and chest trouble, and the taking of various drugs. After the anaesthetic, the patient should be accompanied by a responsible adult.

ALTERNATIVE METHODS OF PAIN CONTROL

Pain can be controlled by *hypnosis*. The word is derived from the Greek *hypnos* meaning 'sleep' and the term was coined in the 1840s by a Scottish surgeon, James Braid. It was thought to have miraculous powers and it is likely that some aspects of witchcraft probably have a link with hypnosis. Hypnosis is a useful tool in dental surgery and it is unfortunate that its development was held up by its association with quackery.

The Austrian physician, Franz Anton Mesmer (1734–1815), found that some people attending his 'seances' appeared healed after he had waved magnets over them. It was then found that it was enough for people only to drink water over which he had passed a magnet. In Paris a Commission, which included the American diplomat, Benjamin Franklin (1706–90), and the French chemist, Antoine Laurent Lavoisier (1743–94), was set up to investigate his claims. In 1784, the Commission concluded that no 'magnetic fluid' existed and that the miraculous cures claimed to have been effected by Mesmer were due to imagination. They did not, however, deny that people had been cured.

Again, in about 1840, John Elliotson in London used hypnotism to practise surgery, including leg amputations, painlessly. Braid, however, separated the science of hypnosis from mesmerism and introduced the concept of monoideism, which is concerned with concentrating the focus of attention on one subject to the exclusion of all others. Even the Austrian psychoanalyst, Sigmund Freud (1856–1939), used hypnosis to treat some neurotic disorders. And, during the two World Wars, hypnosis was used in treating people suffering from the effects of shell shock and other neuroses. The earlier work resulted in the formulation of hypnosis as a state of hypersuggestibility, although there still remains no satisfactory theory of how hypnosis actually works.

The hypnotic state was a result of belief, misdirected attention, and expectation. In other words, it is an artificial state, resembling deep sleep, in which the person who has been hypnotized becomes involuntarily and unconsciously obedient to suggestions made by the hypnotist. Not everyone is susceptible to hypnosis, however, and anyone who is sceptical about its effects is less likely to be induced into a hypnotic state.

Hypnosis is not always successful in relieving pain, and its success does depend on the individual's pain threshold in the first place, but it can work very well so that even the most anxious person may allow surgery to be performed. It will help to eliminate stress and tension and allow the dentist to give an injection, for example, because the patient believes that it will not hurt. Indeed, cases have been reported in which teeth have actually been extracted with no other form of anaesthesia than hypnosis. Hypnosis can be particularly valuable in treating painlessly patients whose medical histories suggest that other, more conventional, anaesthetic techniques may not be advisable. Some patients worry about being placed in a hypnotic state in the belief that they will do or say something which they would not normally do and which may be embarrassing. It is unlikely, however, that anyone will do anything that is not normally in their nature. There is a London-based society, the British Society of Medical and Dental Hypnosis, to which some dentists belong, that encourages the use of hypnosis in dentistry.

The suggestions of the hypnotist seem to be effective using a soft, monotonous voice describing scenes which allow a freedom of movement yet concentrate on one subject, such as a floating balloon. Really what is happening is that a focus of attention is being created to the exclusion of all other subjects. Under these circumstances, the pain threshold of the subject is modified, and many dentists have found that their patients show an increased pain threshold even under light hypnosis. Hypnotism is rarely used in major surgery but its use does enhance the effects of certain drugs. It can be used in childbirth and in the control of pain for untreatable terminal cancer patients. As well as for pain control, in dentistry, it is useful in suppressing the gagging reflexes and in helping people to adapt to new dentures.

As a science, hypnosis, like anaesthesia generally, is still in its infancy but the possibilities for its advancement are interesting and exciting. Unfortunately, however, because of its theatrical origins, the science of hypnosis has suffered a certain amount of ridicule. But, more will be learned about its function and effects as the pathways in the brain and the workings of the mind are uncovered. You must never try to practise hypnosis on one another but the use of suggestion should not be underrated. It may be particularly important in treating children. For example, if a child is told that the dentist is going to use a drill to prepare a tooth, he or she may expect to feel pain because his or her idea of a drill may be the one that is used to dig up the road. On the other hand, if when the dentist is preparing the tooth for a restoration, you need to explain the procedure, it is a good idea to associate what is happening with something pleasant. If, then, the dentist uses an instrument which creates a fine spray that is cold, like ice cream, try to persuade the child to think of the ice cream rather than about dentists' drills.

⑨ MEDICAL CONDITIONS AND DENTISTRY

There is increasing evidence that gum disease is a factor in the development of heart disease and diabetes.

Some medical conditions, and the drugs that you may already be taking, as well as past medications or illnesses to which you have been subjected may have a significant bearing on any dental treatment that is planned for you. Some drugs, for example, interact with others that the dentist may use. Therefore, it is vitally important that you provide your dentist with a concise and accurate record of your current ailments or medications. Your dentist will treat this information in complete confidence and you should provide it freely.

You may be surprised by some of the questions that your dentist asks you because they may not seem relevant to dental treatment, but the diversity of problems which can affect the teeth and gums, as well as the treatment, is so wide that perhaps no-one knows the full implications of some conditions. So don't be shy; tell your dentist everything you know about your state of health. Some people are especially reticent about particular aspects of their health, such as sexually transmitted diseases, taking the contraceptive pill, taking antidepressant drugs, or even pregnancy. But it is important that your dentist should know about these subjects as we will discuss later in the chapter.

HEART CONDITIONS – RHEUMATIC FEVER

This disease usually occurs in children between the ages of five and fifteen years and often follows a severe sore throat which has been caused by the bacteria streptococci. Rheumatic fever is referred to as an auto-immune disease which means that the body's reaction to infection is directed against normal, healthy body cells as well as against the affected ones. In the case of rheumatic fever, the joints and, sometimes, the heart valves may be damaged and, after the acute stage of the disease, the affected valves may remain damaged. The surfaces of the valves become roughened and the smooth flow of blood through the heart may be impeded, resulting in a heart murmur (abnormal heart sound).

Not every case of rheumatic fever will result in damage to the heart valves but you must tell your dentist if you have ever suffered from rheumatic fever because it is possible that, during dental procedures, such as the extraction of teeth, scaling, or extensive restorative treatment, the bacteria which normally live in the mouth may gain access to the bloodstream. Once they have entered into the circulatory system, these bacteria can set up infections in and around the heart valves. This may result in a serious, and possibly fatal, condition called endocarditis, which means an infection of the inner walls of the heart. Once this stage has been reached, using antibiotics may not be effective. Provided your dentist is aware of your condition, however, the problem can be avoided by the administration of antibiotics, such as penicillin or clindamycin before dental treatment. In this way, the bacteria will be destroyed in the bloodstream before they can infect the heart valves and walls. At the time of writing (July 2006), however, there is increasing evidence that dental procedures, such as scaling and extractions as mentioned above, may not, in fact, lead to infections in the heart from migrating bacteria from the mouth, even in susceptible patients. The risk of contracting infections of this kind has to be balanced against the risk of allergic reaction to any antibiotics used to treat infection. It has been stated that there is a 13.5-times greater risk of having an allergic reaction to the antibiotic than of contracting a heart infection. Your dentist should be fully aware of this new evidence and will advise you accordingly.

There are other conditions affecting the heart which your dentist should know about. These include congenital defects, such as a hole in the heart, Sydenham's chorea (St Vitus's Dance), and, of course, any history of heart operations, particularly the placement of artificial valves or pacemakers. Conversely, patients who are about to undergo heart surgery should certainly have a thorough dental examination and should be fully instructed in oral hygiene as part of their treatment.

THE BLOOD

An adult weighing about 70 kilograms (11 stones) has about 5 litres (8 pints) of blood coursing through the veins and arteries. Blood carries nutrients to various parts of the body and, in particular, conveys oxygen from the lungs to those tissues, such as muscles and the brain, which need the oxygen to be able to function. The oxygen is carried by the red blood cells in the blood, combining with the haemoglobin to form oxy-haemoglobin. It is the arterial blood which carries the oxygen while the blood flowing through the veins carries blood back to the heart once it has given up its oxygen. Obviously, any interference with the oxygen-carrying capacity of the blood is important. In dentistry, care must be taken when antibiotics are administered because these drugs may reduce the amount of oxygen which is available to the body and, therefore, your dentist must be aware if you suffer from any conditions, such as anaemia, which result in a low level of haemoglobin. Indeed, if your dentist feels that you need to be treated under a general anaesthetic, he or she may insist that you have a blood test first to make sure that your haemoglobin level and red blood cell count are normal.

Patients from Africa, the West Indies, Asia, or from Mediterranean areas may suffer from sickle cell anaemia and they should always be willing to have a specific blood test to check for this condition. Any reduction in oxygen in this condition may cause the blood cells to change from the normal saucer shape to a sickle shape, seriously reducing their capacity to carry oxygen and ultimately causing the cells to rupture. When this takes place, the bone marrow is unable to replace the red cells quickly enough and the condition may result in rapid death. Consequently, any procedures which may lower the potential oxygen which is available should be carried out only after testing for sickle cell anaemia. Of course, it is reassuring anyway, to know that your dentist has a record of whether you are sickle cell positive or negative, especially if you have to undergo dental or surgical procedures in the future. Patients should also be tested before any sedative techniques are used.

In 1925, Cooley and Lee described a severe type of anaemia called thalassaemia. Many of the patients were of Mediterranean origin and the disease is characterized by a decrease in the rate of production of the oxygen-carrying pigment, haemoglobin. The type of haemoglobin varies from the normal. The patients exhibit bone changes (bossing – enlargement of some skull bones) which may result in a malocclusion. The patients also seem to have an increased predisposition to infection. The disease leads to problems when the availability of oxygen is diminished, as may be the case under general anaesthesia.

You will have gathered that your dentist should know if you are suffering from any kind of anaemia. The elderly, the pregnant woman, or the nursing mother may be anaemic.

Haemophilia is an inherited blood disorder in which the blood's ability to clot is impaired so that even minor wounds bleed uncontrollably. It affects about six people in every 100,000. Haemophilia arises because the body is unable to produce a substance called blood factor 8 which is referred to as anti-haemophiliac globulin or AHG. Other factors responsible for blood clotting may also be deficient as is the case in patients suffering from a condition known as Christmas Disease. Patients suffering from these diseases can be treated, usually in hospital, by the administration of particular blood factors. Obviously, extracting teeth from haemophiliacs is likely to be hazardous and best avoided, so that dental disorders should be prevented, if at all possible, and it is vital that these patients should be thoroughly instructed in good oral hygiene techniques.

A blood test may also reveal deficiencies in the white blood cells which are largely responsible for the control of infection in the body. It is also possible that the body may be producing many abnormal immature white blood cells, which is one of the characteristics of leukaemia, a disease that may show other symptoms in the mouth. Severe ulceration and bleeding of the gums are most likely to be the result of poor oral hygiene but, if these problems persist in a clean mouth, they should be investigated promptly.

THE LUNGS

Sometimes, lung infections can give rise to halitosis (bad breath) and your dentist might well bear this in mind if you complain that you are suffering from this embarrassing condition because, in the absence of dental disease, it is a likely cause of the problem. We have already mentioned the importance of anaemia when anaesthetics are administered and, similarly, the efficiency of the lungs is of paramount importance in the absorption of oxygen. Therefore, you should always tell your dentist if you have recently had a bad cough, cold, influenza, or any other chest infection, such as tuberculosis, pleurisy, or pneumonia. Obviously, if you were suffering from one of these diseases, you would be unlikely to have a general anaesthetic for dental work but, if your dentist is aware of the situation, it might well influence any decision that the dentist or anaesthetist may come to for future treatment.

DISABLEMENT

Mental handicap presents a particular problem in dental treatment because today's dentistry does depend largely on communication between dentist and patient. Therefore, any mentally handicapped person must be made aware, if at all possible, of the importance of good preventive measures. This aspect of prevention is dependent mainly on strengthening the enamel, that is, by fluoridation administered both systemically (in water or tablet form) and topically by the application of gels, and on the control of the sugar, particularly sucrose, in the diet of the handicapped person. Often mentally handicapped children and adults are treated under general anaesthetic and, although it is not uncommon for general dental practitioners to treat such patients, many are dealt with in a hospital environment.

Brain damage after an accident may result in mental as well as physical handicap. In the case of a physically handicapped person, the electric toothbrush may well prove to be very useful and people with orthopaedic injuries should be reminded that, with limited hand movements, the maintenance of good oral hygiene may require additional time and effort.

The brain may be damaged when a blood clot blocks a blood vessel supplying part of the brain. This is commonly referred to as a stroke. The side of the face may be partially paralysed as well as the hand and leg on one side of the body. Obviously, food debris is likely to accumulate in the sulcus of the mouth on that side due to lack of tongue and lip movement. When the patient has recovered sufficiently, this should be pointed out so that additional effort to clean the area can be made.

Depression, as a result of a stressful situation such as severe domestic problems, may result in bruxism (grinding of the teeth) and a lack of personal hygiene which may cause an increase in tooth decay and gum disease. It is possible that social workers can help here by bringing the problem to the attention of such a person if the situation permits.

In the case of the condition known as hydrocephalus, where the fluid surrounding the brain does not drain away normally, a special device or shunt may be fitted to aid the drainage. As with artificial heart valves, these appliances may encourage the stagnation of bacteria and the patient may need to be treated with antibiotics before any dental work is carried out. Again, all such children must be taught good oral hygiene and the sugar intake should be controlled.

In epilepsy, part of the brain is damaged, although this does not infer a reduced mental capacity. Epileptics are often treated using a drug called phenytoin sodium, which has the unfortunate side effect of causing the fibrous tissue parts of the gums to enlarge, possibly requiring corrective surgery. On the other hand, periodontal specialists generally feel that, if plaque is properly controlled, epileptics are less likely to require this form of treatment.

THE NERVOUS SYSTEM

There are some disorders of the nervous system which diminish a person's response to pain. For example, a child with chronically carious teeth but with no apparent pain may be a sufferer, although this condition is rare. A much more common and localized condition is Bell's Palsy, first described by Sir Charles Bell (1774–1842) whose book, *Nervous Systems of the Human Body*, published in 1830, was well received by his contemporaries. Bell's Palsy usually affects one of the facial nerves which supply the muscles of facial expression in one side of the face. This condition can arise quite suddenly and may be distressing. Sometimes, the palsy is caused by pressure on the nerve from injury, tumour, or infection but, more commonly, it arises spontaneously as in true Bell's Palsy.

If you are affected by the condition, you should visit your medical practitioner straight away so that anti-inflammatory drugs, known as steroids, may be prescribed for you. It seems that the quicker the treatment is begun, the shorter the time that the nerve is affected and a return to normal is possible. Patient's suffering from Bell's Palsy may drool saliva from the corner of the mouth and the lip may droop on one side, but the dentist should be able to help here if the patient is a denture wearer by increasing the bulk of the denture to give more support to the cheek. Even where the natural dentition is present, the dentist can fit an appliance to the cheek side of the teeth on the affected side which carries a roll of plastic to support the cheek. The patients gain great comfort from the improvement to their appearance, so a trip to the dentist may be invaluable.

THE KIDNEYS

The kidneys assist in the excretion from the body of certain toxic waste products. Persistently taking drugs may damage the kidneys and, indeed, paracetamol, aspirin, and caffeine have all been implicated if they are taken over a prolonged period. Older people, in particular, may suffer from impaired kidney function so that the dosages of any drugs may need to be modified to take this into account. Patients on dialysis machines may be fitted with arteriovenous shunts to assist the fixing of tubes to the veins and arteries. These shunts may be left attached after dialysis and, as in the case of the shunts used in the treatment of hydrocephalus, they may become a hiding place for bacteria.

A dentist may provide antibiotic cover for these patients as a precaution in case the dental procedure itself results in the introduction of bacteria into the bloodstream. In these circumstances this would almost certainly be carried out in conjunction with advice from the patient's physician.

THE LIVER

The liver destroys toxins and helps to remove waste products from the body. One particular transmissible disease, hepatitis, is especially hazardous to your dentist, staff, and other patients. The virus which causes the disease may be found in saliva as well as in blood and many patients suffering from hepatitis are treated in special centres. Drug addicts may contract hepatitis from using dirty needles, and there is probably a case for compulsory registration of all tattoo artists and ear-piercing clinics to ensure that proper sterilization of equipment is carried out. Alcohol, too, affects the liver resulting in a condition known as cirrhosis, and past and present alcoholics may suffer from liver damage. If you know that you have been affected in this way, you must tell your dentist because any future drug therapy or treatment may need to be modified.

AIDS

We wrote in 1986 that 'It has been reported that the virus associated with the Acquired Immune Deficiency Syndrome is occasionally present in saliva'. This has now been proven, as has the fact that it is also certainly present in blood. There are now strict guidelines recommended by the British Dental Association and General Dental Council regarding the control of cross-infection in the dental surgery.

It is most important that you inform your dentist if you have suffered from any infectious disease and this is especially true of hepatitis and AIDS (acquired immuno-deficiency syndrome) caused by HIV (human immuno-deficiency virus). Some patients who have not developed full-blown AIDS may be carriers and said to be HIV positive – such patients must also inform their dental practitioner. At the time of writing, there is no cure for AIDS but there is a great deal of research being carried out and we must hope that a cure will be forthcoming.

There are set regimes for treatment of all patients whether or not they may be HIV positive. The guidelines on cross-infection control protect everybody and are welcomed by members of the dental profession. It is not only an 'HIV' issue but applies to other communicable diseases such as hepatitis.

Nowadays, most dental practitioners, their surgery assistants, and dental hygienists each wears a new pair of disposable gloves when treating every patient. They may also wear protective eye goggles to limit mechanical injury as well as infection. In addition, most practices sterilize all instruments in an autoclave (a high-pressure steam cooker) and the autoclave itself must be inspected and maintained at three-monthly intervals.

In 1994 a Panorama report on BBC television drew attention to a case in the United States in which it was alleged that the HIV had been passed to a young patient from a dentist because there had been a lack of proper cross-infection control. The report therefore sought to point out that, while the risk was small, there is no room for complacency on this issue. In some respects, this kind of reporting is to be welcomed although it did give rise to some alarm among the general public.

Dentists are advised that, without exception, all instruments should be adequately cleaned and sterilized between patients. It has been suggested that, because many dental drills (handpieces) are more liable to fail if they are repeatedly sterilized, there should be greater government funding to allow dentists working within the NHS to acquire more handpieces so that there is less wear and tear on each one. In some areas, funds have been made available for this purpose.

Private dentists, working outside the NHS, also follow the General Dental Council's guidelines on cross-infection control and take full responsibility for such control. Organizations, such as Denplan and British United Provident Association (BUPA), are particularly keen that all practitioners should adhere to the accepted guidelines.

If you have any doubts about any of the procedures carried out at the dental practice you attend, ask the dentist for reassurance and perhaps even to show you how cross-infection controls are implemented. It is just as important for HIV-positive patients to gain such assurances as it is for healthy patients. The usual system is that HIV-positive patients are treated at the end of the day or when there is sufficient time prior to the arrival of the next patient to ensure that disinfection procedures can be carried out thoroughly and effectively. It must be said that, if a dentist admits to being unwilling to treat HIV-positive patients because the cross-infection controls are inadequate, then other blood-borne infections could also be transmitted so that the practice should reappraise its own policies and procedures. This is a continuing debate, however, with many finer points of contention and, where treatment in special centres is possible for HIV-positive patients, then it would be best if they made use of them.

Good oral hygiene procedures are of course immensely important for persons whose immune systems are compromised in any way, and, while this may not be at the forefront of their minds, much discomfort can be avoided by sound dental health advice. With the proper care, however, risks are greatly diminished and with proper understanding, they may well be eliminated. In a practice of, say, 3000 patients it is quite possible that at least one person carries a communicable disease without knowing it so we cannot overemphasize the importance of strict cross-infection controls at all times. In fact, general dental practitioners, with guidance from the British Dental Association and the General Dental Council, have been at the forefront of cross-infection control and have much cause to be proud of their record.

And, of course, it is worth remembering that it may be the dentist looking in your mouth who spots the tell-tale signs of a general illness.

DIABETES

Diabetics are no more prone to tooth decay and gum disease than any other individuals but their healing capacity after injury or disease may be affected. Oral hygiene instruction and dietary control go hand in hand so there is every reason for a diabetic to be fully familiar with the methods of preventive dentistry.

PREGNANCY

Most doctors of medicine and dentists agree that general anaesthetics, medications of any sort, and surgery or radiological procedures should be avoided for pregnant women patients. Local anaesthetics can be used, however, and some dentists recommend the use of a type which does not contain any adrenaline. It is during the first and final stages of pregnancy that medication in particular should be avoided and it is generally agreed that the middle three-month period is a safer time to provide treatment if it is essential. Antibiotics and tranquillizers should be rigorously avoided.

As almost every woman knows, pregnancy itself affects the hormone balance of her body. Such hormonal changes may possibly lead to an increased tendency towards gum disease although, if plaque build-up is properly controlled, this should not be a serious problem. Sometimes, however, the gum in a localized area may become extremely overgrown, resulting in a 'pregnancy epulis'. An epulis refers to any swelling on the gum and such may require removal surgically. The pregnancy epulis may disappear spontaneously after the birth of the child. If it is removed surgically it is easily carried out under local anaesthesia.

Anaemia, stress, and possibly morning sickness during pregnancy are factors to which more attention should be paid. Morning sickness may result in the regurgitation into the mouth of food from the stomach. This can have a damaging affect on the teeth because the regurgitated stomach contents are very acidic. Therefore, the mouth should be cleaned and rinsed after any episode of vomiting, including the eating disorder bulimia.

THE MENOPAUSE

Menstruation in women generally ceases between the ages of 45 and 55 years and may result in some oral symptoms such as a dry mouth or ulceration of the gums and other mucous membranes that line the mouth cavity. Abnormal taste patterns may also develop. These conditions may lead to extreme discomfort and difficulty in wearing dentures. Of course a dry mouth also indicates a reduced flow of saliva so that acidity in the mouth may not be neutralized and decay of the tooth enamel may begin. Your dentist might suggest that hormone replacement therapy (HRT) prescribed by your medical practitioner could be useful. Local treatment of the condition may only be palliative. Owing to psychological disturbance at this time a woman may habitually and painfully grind her teeth in her sleep – nocturnal bruxism. A bite guard may prove useful here.

ULCERS

An ulcer is a break in the skin or other lining material of the body. Such a lesion in the stomach, for example, is referred to as a gastric ulcer and may result from excess acidity eroding the stomach lining or, more recently, it has been suggested that it is caused by a bacterium or virus. In the mouth, small ulcers, which can be extremely painful in the early stages, often develop at times of stress, such as during menstruation, and young girls beginning menstruation frequently experience ulceration of the tongue, cheeks, and gums. Any young person taking school examinations or starting a new job may suffer from ulcers, and adults can be affected, too. These aphthous ulcers, as they are called, have a yellowish surface with a raised and inflamed edge. They are rarely more than 0.5 centimetre long and are quite harmless, lasting for about eight days. An ulcer which persists for more than about a week, however, should be examined by your dentist or doctor. If you are particularly prone to ulceration of the mouth, you may get some relief from the application of an antiseptic gel to its surface; or your doctor or dentist may prescribe an anti-inflammatory drug to ease the condition. In any case, you certainly won't drown your fish and chips in vinegar!

Cold sores are caused by the herpes virus which may also affect other parts of the body. The virus lies dormant within the cells of the body, and it is only when you are subjected to further stress or illness that the familiar cold sore on the lips appears. When you first feel the typical burning sensation, it is well worth paying a visit to your doctor or dentist because you may be able to avoid the full effects of a cold sore by applying a medication to your lips when it first begins. Children sometimes suffer from a primary herpes infection which may affect the whole of the lining of the mouth. The gums often become red and painful, and many ulcers break out in the mouth. The child should rest in bed, and doctors and dentists usually recommend a diet of soft, nutritious foods which are low in sucrose – this is not an occasion for lack of plaque control! This condition should last only two or three days at most, and mouthwashes are often prescribed to prevent bacteria from infecting the ulcerated surfaces of the mouth.

A word of warning seems in order here. If you find that you have any kind of swelling or lumps and bumps in your mouth, or anywhere else for that matter, don't just sit back and hope they will go away. Seek medical or dental advice straight away. Not every little lump that appears spontaneously is likely to be dangerous but it is better to be safe than sorry; prompt treatment can even save lives in some cases.

SPEECH DEFECTS

Children who lisp or who have some other speech impediment may also benefit from good dental care. Speech therapists are fully aware that certain sounds cannot be made properly without the use of the teeth, and dental defects, such as an open bite, will cause a speech difficulty. Underdevelopment of the lower jaw, for example, may result in the child having a lisp.

Denture wearers, also, may only be too aware of the effects of restricted tongue space on their speech patterns, and anyone who plays a musical wind instrument may find it difficult to cope with dentures. Fortunately, there are dentists who specialize in dental care for musicians but any budding wind instrumentalist or singer would do well to know about the way in which dental disease can play havoc with the voice or with the embouchure (the correct application of the lips and tongue in playing).

The voice is also dependent upon the bones around the face because spaces within them, called sinuses, affect its resonance. Anyone who has suffered with a heavy head cold knows what it is like to speak with that 'blocked-up' feeling. The sinuses in the upper jaw bones are very large. These sinuses can fill with mucus and inflammatory fluids causing the pressure within the sinus to be raised slightly. The lining of the sinus is close to the surface of the upper molars so that, when this happens, any movements of the head may cause pain in the teeth. This condition is known as sinusitis. The sinus in the upper jaw is also referred to as the antrum, and it increases in size as the jaws develop. When an upper molar tooth is extracted, the dentist must be very careful not to push its roots into the antrum although, even if this does occur, it can still be retrieved but it requires a special surgical approach.

AGEING

Father time is no respecter of dental tissues, and older people may be presented with particular dental problems. We have already mentioned that kidney function is impaired in the elderly and that prescribing drugs is only undertaken with caution.

Over the years, tooth enamel is worn down by attrition, and the individual's diet is perhaps the most important factor in the wear process. This wearing away of the enamel can occur at the contact points because, in time, the teeth may move slightly and rub against one another. Indeed, it has been reported that a 1-centimetre loss in the length of the dental arch can occur by the age of forty years.

Dentine continues to be produced throughout life and this has the effect of narrowing the pulp canals of the teeth. This makes root canal therapy (endodontic treatment) particularly difficult in the elderly. The extra dentine is called secondary dentine and is common in the aged. The tubules in the dentine may become sealed at one end and appear opaque to transmitted light. This has the effect of making the teeth look darker.

The pulp of the tooth changes with age. Sometimes, a pulp stone, which is a calcified nodule in the pulp canal or chamber, is seen. These pose problems for endodontic procedures.

The cementum, which covers the roots of the teeth, may increase with age but gum disease and the stresses of mastication may hinder its production. Sometimes, cementum becomes so abundant that extraction of a tooth becomes hazardous and a surgical approach is therefore necessary. It is wise to have radiographic pictures taken before a tooth is extracted if people are beyond middle age.

Becoming 'long in the tooth' is not entirely avoidable but it is likely that good oral hygiene throughout life, carefully planned dental treatment, and adequate nutrition may well result in a slowing down of the ageing effects in the gum and periodontal fibres, particularly by reducing stress in the biting surfaces of the teeth. Examination of teeth gives some indication of age, and forensic scientists often use dental evidence to ascertain the ages of unidentified corpses. Wear patterns, pulp chamber thickness, and the colour changes in the dental tissues are used in the process of identification.

ARTIFICIAL JOINTS

Artificial joints, such as hip replacements, may provide a site for bacteria to lodge. Because bacteria may enter the blood stream in dental surgery, it is necessary, therefore, in some cases, to provide antibiotic cover for such patients before treatment. Though arthritis and rheumatism are not necessarily associated with old age, it is worth remembering that oral hygiene is affected by lack of manual dexterity.

HEREDITARY AND BIRTH DEFECTS AFFECTING TEETH AND JAWS

During the development of the face in the embryo, defects may occur which result in the formation of clefts, and lead to conditions such as a cleft palate or a hare lip. There is no evidence, however, that children suffering from these problems have weaker teeth or gums than others. Because they are diagnosed immediately nowadays, treatment to repair defects of this kind will often be started soon after birth. The growth of the teeth and jaws must be constantly supervised so that the right sort of corrective surgery and orthodontic treatment can be provided at the most suitable time. In the late 1970s, a breakthrough was made in detecting accurately changes which occur in body structure. Professor Peter Burke of Sheffield and Dr Leonard Beard of Cambridge University pioneered a system which can map, quite clearly, curves of the human body to an accuracy of 0.5 millimetre. In this way, a series of pictures can show how the soft tissue of the face can alter over a period of time, as well as indicating the effects of any corrective procedures.

Measles, chicken pox, or any other bacterial or viral infection can upset the development of the teeth. Fortunately, however, any teeth that have been affected in this way can be crowned or coated with a veneer of tooth-coloured, plastic-like material, such as those used in the acid-etching technique mentioned in Chapter 3.

MEDICINES

We have mentioned medicines elsewhere in the text but it is as well to be reminded that medicines which have been highly sweetened with sucrose are to be avoided if possible. Medication in pregnancy, in the elderly, and in those suffering from kidney and liver disease needs careful consideration. Some drugs affect the teeth of an unborn child. The antibiotic drug, tetracycline, crosses the placenta and causes yellow staining of teeth and bone. The approximate age at which the drug was administered can be determined from the position of the yellow band on the teeth which were forming at the time. Tetracycline is best avoided during pregnancy for this reason alone. Both first and second teeth may show staining for no apparent reason but, if there is a defect which stretches across several teeth, it is usually related to some interference in the growth and calcification process of the teeth.

Another drug of interest, particularly to the mother-to-be, is metronidazole (an antibacterial and antifungal), which is often

I am a patient on –

STEROID

TREATMENT

which must not be

stopped abruptly

and in the case of intercurrent

illness may have to be increased

INSTRUCTIONS

1 DO NOT STOP taking the steroid drug except on medical advice. Always have a supply in reserve.

2 In case of feverish illness, accident, operation (emergency or otherwise), diarrhoea or vomiting, the steroid treatment MUST be continued. Your doctor may wish you to have a LARGER DOSE or an INJECTION at such times.

3 If the tablets cause indigestion, consult your doctor AT ONCE.

4 Always carry this card while receiving steroid treatment and show it to any doctor, dentist, nurse, or midwife whom you may consult.

5 After your treatment has finished, you must still tell any new doctor, dentist, nurse, or midwife that you have had steroid treatment

Fig. 28   A Steroid Warning Card (*Crown Copyright, reproduced with the kind permission of the Controller of Her Majesty's Stationery Office.*)

prescribed for gum infections and in post-operative care. This drug is partially secreted in breast milk and will therefore be passed on to the newborn child who clearly does not need it.

You should keep a record of all long-term medication and particularly steroids, anticoagulants, and drugs used in some mental disorders, such as mono-amine oxidase inhibitors and tricyclic antidepressant drugs. If you are taking any of these drugs, your medical practitioner will issue you with a blue card, such as the one illustrated in Figure 28. You must show these cards to your dentist and you should inform him or her if you have used the drugs within the previous two years.

If you do require dental treatment, it is possible that the dosage of steroids may need to be increased. Antidepressant drugs may interact with some of the adrenaline-like compounds in local and general anaesthetics. They are surprisingly widely used. Indeed, a recent report stated that one in five women and one in ten men take some kind of tranquillizer, and a total of twenty-five million prescriptions for drugs, such as diazepam (Valium), chlordiazepoxide (Librium), and nitrazepam (Mogadon), are issued every year.

THE CONTRACEPTIVE PILL

The contraceptive pill inhibits ovulation and, therefore, it disrupts the hormonal balance of the body. A girl may experience an increase in breast size, for instance, while taking the pill. The gums may be more susceptible to irritation by plaque in such a person, just as they are in pregnancy. It has been reported that the prescribing of some antibiotics may affect the efficacy of the contraceptive pill – this book is concerned with 'prevention' so don't forget to tell your dentist if you are taking the pill!

MALIGNANCY – CANCER

It has been reported that approximately 2000 new cases of fatal mouth cancer are reported each year. The risk factors are: drinking alcohol; smoking; poor nutrition. The prevalence of mouth cancer is increasing in young people whereas, originally, it was more common in older people. Early detection is of paramount importance and your dentist is ideally placed to detect problems. Remember, it is not only your teeth that he or she is caring for but your whole mouth.

One of the treatments for malignant conditions is radiotherapy and the treatment itself has a bearing on the delivery of dental care. Consequently, if you have had radiotherapy treatment to the head or neck, it is very important to avoid the need for dental surgery. Radiotherapy also affects the salivary glands. You may, therefore, experience a dry mouth as the production and flow of saliva, which tends to neutralize mouth acids, are reduced by the radiotherapy. There is, therefore, a greater risk of tooth decay. Mouthwashes may be helpful in reducing this risk and, because they often contain glycerine and thymol, your mouth will feel much more comfortable, too.

On the other hand, radiotherapy can actually be used to treat malignant disease of the jaws, tongue, lips, cheeks, and gums. At this point, it seems appropriate to mention again the risks associated with drinking alcohol and smoking. Smoking, drinking alcohol, or even eating highly spiced foods may not necessarily cause cancer of the soft tissues of the mouth, but a malignant change can certainly be exacerbated further by these habits. There is, for example, a higher incidence of lip cancer among pipe smokers and there also seems to be a combined effect to increase the risk of cancer to those who smoke and also drink alcohol to excess.

If you smoke a pipe, it may be a good idea to inspect your mouth using a mouth mirror from time to time. You may notice that the roof of your mouth becomes very white and that small red dots appear. This is caused by the tiny glands in the roof of the mouth becoming blocked by the overproduction of the material keratin. The condition is called smoker's keratosis. It is not in itself a malignant condition and very few cases become so. You should, however, immediately cut down on your smoking and seek medical or dental advice. It is a sign that your smoking habit is affecting the health of your mouth. Even malignant conditions can be treated successfully if they are caught in time, so don't hesitate. Seek advice about any lumps or bumps or changes in the coloration of the lips, tongue, and cheek surfaces. The dental check-up is the only screening programme – make use of the service.

It has been reported that the Bangladeshi community in Britain is at a much higher risk of developing mouth cancer because of the prevalence among Bangladeshis of the habit of chewing tobacco or betel (plug, quid). The charity, Cancer Research UK, is endeavouring to highlight this growing problem. Increased numbers of cases of mouth cancer are also being reported among the population in general, however. This is almost certainly linked to an increase in smoking and the growing trend of binge drinking. It has long been known that excessive spirit drinking combined with smoking greatly increase the risk of mouth cancer. This is a particularly worrying phenomenon because it is among the young that these increases are occurring.

If left undetected, mouth cancer may be fatal.
If mouth cancer is detected early, treatment is remarkably successful.

Malignant disease of the tongue, lips, and cheeks can be fatal, and it is of paramount importance that mouth cancer is detected early. Your dentist can provide an early diagnosis and can help you to get prompt advice and treatment. You can also look in your own mouth and be aware of the following symptoms:

1 a sore spot or ulcer that has not healed within, say, seven days;
2 a change in colour of any part of your mouth and, for example, a red spot or white patch;
3 persistent sore throat or croaky voice;
4 pain on swallowing;
5 enlarged glands in your neck;
6 pain in your mouth, tongue, or ears.

Do not be alarmed if you have any of the symptoms listed above – the chances are very high that you do **not** have cancer. But the important thing is, you must seek professional advice quickly. Remember, ignorance is not bliss, ignorance may be fatal!

FAINTING

Generally speaking, most people regard all dental treatment as an ordeal, although it should be no more so than any other kind of surgery. Perhaps it is the thought of the invasion of the mouth with needles and other paraphernalia which causes so much anxiety. In any case, fainting in the dental surgery cannot be considered to be a rare occurrence. It is caused by a temporary fall in blood pressure, possibly brought on by fear. Provided a faint is not prolonged, the patient should come to little or no harm but, if you know that you are prone to fainting at the sight of blood or a needle, then you should make sure that you are accompanied when you go for dental treatment. Certainly, if you have to have transport to reach the surgery and you are a car driver, don't be tempted to drive yourself home afterwards. Either arrange for a taxi to collect you or ask someone to accompany you on public transport. Your judgement may be impaired after a faint, so don't take any chances.

SNORING

Snoring, we are told, is quite common: about 20 per cent of men and 10 per cent of women snore. Some people might find the idea of snoring amusing but the effect on the snorer can be serious, and partners of snorers may find it hard to sleep. If, for example, your powers of concentration lapse during the day or, indeed, if you feel tired earlier that you should, then it may be that you have a sleep problem associated with snoring. Snoring can cause blood oxygen levels to fall significantly, and this may lead to serious medical, or even social, consequences as a result of your daytime lack of concentration. If you drive a motor vehicle or operate heavy machinery, tiredness can, literally, be fatal for you or for someone else, so you must seek advice.

You may be wondering why snoring should get a mention in a book on dental health. When a person is sleeping, the posture of the mouth and the tongue is under less control, and a dentist is ideally placed to make appliances that can reduce the effects of snoring considerably.

Snoring is related to the opening of a person's airway. The problem occurs when the muscles relax during sleep and, if a person is overweight, the condition may be exacerbated so that the increase in obesity among the population at large will lead to snoring becoming more widespread. It is quite likely, of course, that the snorer is unaware that he or she snores but a tactful comment from a partner may suggest to the person with the problem that he or she should seek advice

The first person that a snorer should consult is his or her GP to determine the severity of the condition. If the practitioner recommends that an 'anti-snoring device' should be used, the dentist is ideally placed to take impressions and to oversee the fitting of the appliance. These anti-snoring devices alter the position of the lower jaw during sleep, thereby helping to keep the airway open and thus reduce the snoring.

EATING DISORDERS

Anorexia and bulimia result in reguritation of acid into the mouth, which can damage the enamel of the teeth. If you suffer from these conditions, discuss the matter with your dentist, who may advise you on how to limit the damage.

CHANGING YOUR DENTIST

Multiple surgery practices may engage the services of different dentists. We feel that it is important that you record the name of the dentists that have treated you and check that the new dentist is aware of any past medication and your medical condition. This particular aspect of dental care is quite worrying to patients and many do not like to see a succession of locums, associates, and assistants. This is quite understandable but often unavoidable. The advantages are that you may get the benefit of various opinions but the overriding disadvantage is a possible lack of continuity of care and that your new dentist may not initially be aware of your particular needs. With thorough questioning by the dentist and a patient freely giving personal information, the problem diminishes.

IN CONCLUSION

To practise dentistry, a person must be highly trained as well as having a wide knowledge of health care in general. Therefore, you can do a lot to help your dentist and yourself by remembering that the teeth should not and cannot be treated in isolation from the rest of the body. It is worth repeating that every tooth and, indeed, every atom of the body is, to a greater or lesser extent, dependent for its survival on every other part of the body.

Please bear in mind that the information we have included in this chapter is by no means exhaustive because it would need a whole medical textbook to cover the subject fully.

10 FUNDING DENTAL FITNESS

There are, perhaps, as many shades of opinion about how dental health care should be funded as there are dentists and their patients. Here we outline some of the schemes that are available in the United Kingdom. There are other schemes, however, and, as you read this book, there are probably new organizations entering the marketplace.

Some loyal and devoted patients have complete faith and trust in their dentists and, because they are in the fortunate position of being able to meet the likely fees for any treatment, they hardly consider the cost before undertaking it. On the other hand, there are those who, perhaps because of circumstances, lifestyle, or both, need a lot of dental health care but are unable to pay for it. And between, of course, there are many people who demand quality care at a price that they can reasonably easily afford.

For many years, the dental profession in Britain has offered first-class care to everyone who requires it within the various National Health schemes, and many dentists would prefer that there continues to be an adequate, fair, and equitable state-funding system so that the disadvantaged in the community are offered help when they need it. Like all aspects of health care, however, dental techniques and materials are making great leaps forward, and the cost of modern dentistry is outstripping the funding that is usually available for the treatments the dentist thinks are needed. It should be remembered, too, that a dental practice is a small business and, like all small businesses, at the mercy of the ups and downs of economic conditions and market forces.

In any dental practice today, one of the most important, and expensive, procedures is the control of cross-infection as ever-more stringent requirements are applied to all health practitioners. It is probably the cost of these procedures, more than any other single factor, that has forced dentist after dentist to opt for total control over the funding of the practice by becoming private practitioners working independently of a state-run scheme that admits to inadequate resources. While every dentist is perfectly well able to implement the cross-infection controls required to satisfy the standards determined by, for example, the British Dental Association, some dentists cannot install the high standard of control they feel they should within NHS funding.

None of this suggests that a dental practice operating entirely or partly within the National Health Service offers inadequate standards. But many dentists have reached the conclusion that, within the NHS, they are unable to take the time they need to carry out the treatments they deem necessary and still keep up with the overheads of their practices let alone earn a reasonable living. Thus they ask for fees to come direct from their patients at a level high enough to enable them to attain the standards to which they were trained.

It is well known that, in Britain, the cost of living and especially of housing, varies from region to region. Where property is expensive, therefore, a dentist's practice team requires higher salaries than in less expensive areas. But National Health Service funding does not allow for that and the fee paid to the dentist for the patient sitting in the chair remains the same throughout the land. For dentistry within the NHS to continue, this is one problem that must be addressed. At the moment, there seems for the NHS little alternative than to create a system where the State funds all the overheads of the practice.

EXEMPTIONS FROM DENTAL CHARGES

At the time of writing, the following groups of people are exempt from National Health Service charges for dental care.

1 Persons under eighteen years of age.
2 Persons under nineteen years of age and who are in full-time education.
3 Persons claiming Income Support.
4 Pregnant women.
5 Nursing mothers – mothers with children under the age of a year.
6 Persons receiving Job Seeker's allowances.

Note that old age pensioners (senior citizens) are not exempt from National Health Service dental charges.

Where there is no obvious reason for a person to be exempted from dental charges but that person may experience financial difficulties in undergoing a necessary treatment, there is a financial assistance procedure and most general dental practices have the appropriate claim forms. If you are being treated under the National Health Service and you think you have a reasonable claim for financial assistance, do ask the dentist about it. You should also ask the dentist for an estimate of the likely charges but, remember, from a first examination it is not always possible to determine exactly the full extent of the treatment needed so do build in a bit extra. And, of course, even though you might be exempt from charges because you fall within one of the categories listed above, if you break an appointment, the dentist is at liberty to make a charge.

The new National Health Service contract came into operation on 1 April 2006. All patients were deregistered from a dental practice. Dentists were asked to accept the new contract and to work within a specified budget for the next three years. The budget was based on previous dental activity, and the charges (see below) were altered. Many dentists did not sign up to the new contract while others signed up but in dispute. It is likely that more and more practices will become wholly privately funded.

The new fee structure

	April 2006	(March 2006)

Band 1

Examination fee	£15.40	(£5.84)

This new examination fee also includes the cost of radiographs and preventive advice.

Band 2

The above plus minor filling or extensive restorations and root fillings

	£42.40	(about £35 if only one restoration required)

Band 3

Provision of laboratory-based items, for example, one crown

	£189.40	(1 crown £85, up to a maximumof £394)
Multiple crowns	£189.40	

The overall effect would seem to be that the conscientious regular attender pays more and the less conscientious patient pays considerably less. This would also seem to encourage people to neglect their dental health.

FINANCING DENTAL CARE

A recent survey indicated that there were two factors which deterred some people from seeking dental care, whether that care was simply for advice or for treatment. The factors were: fear of pain; and worry about the likely cost of treatment. As the authors hope this book has already shown, you should not worry unduly about pain. Nowadays, dental treatment should not be an ordeal and all dentists are trained to deal caringly with their patients and to keep discomfort to the absolute minimum. And in future, of course, if dental health and care continue to improve in the way that we would all like, there will be much less need for active treatment anyway because most dental disease and disorders are preventable.

When, in 1983, the first edition of this book, then entitled *Have Healthy Teeth and Gums*, was begun, the choice in Britain was quite simple. Either the patient could simply obtain treatment through the National Health Service or she/he could pay privately. In 1986, a new programme which combined routine care and a continuously active commitment to preventing dental disease was introduced by dental practitioner Stephen Noar. Patients pay a monthly fee to the dentist of her/his choice so that almost all dental services likely to be required could be financed within the monthly budget. In addition, insurance for accidents and emergencies was included, and Denplan Care was born.

DENPLAN

At the time of writing, Denplan Care is the most widely used dental capitation scheme in the private sector. It offers the following services:

1 The registered Denplan Care dentist of your choice enters into a personal agreement with you to provide dental care.
2 In consultation with your dentist, you can budget for all your dental needs so that a full, comprehensive service can be provided within the monthly fee. This includes dental examinations, preventive care (including attention by a dental hygienist), some restorative work, any radiographs (X-ray examinations), root canal treatments, the dentist's time spent in preparing and placing crowns and bridgework (provided they have not been excluded in original contract).
3 Your dentist is enrolled on a practice quality programme which involves assessment and adheres to a code of practice that includes commitment to peer review, as well as continuing post-graduate education. We should emphasize, however, that within the National Health Service, any dental work carried out is also subject to examination and review from time to time.
4 In the event of a dispute between you and your Denplan Care dentist, Denplan provides a conciliation/arbitration service.
5 Denplan provides a list of Denplan accredited dental laboratories that also adhere to a code of practice and guarantee their work for one year.
6 Denplan Care includes a supplementary insurance package that covers accidental damage to your teeth; and there is a 24-hour helpline open seven days a week. If you are abroad and have a

dental emergency, the helpline will find a dentist for you – if possible, an English-speaker.

7 Discounts are available for family or group membership of Denplan Care: 5 per cent for two members; 10 per cent for three members – where premiums are being paid on the same direct debit instruction.

To sum up, for a regular, affordable fee, Denplan Care provides you with a full and comprehensive dental care programme, backed up by access to emergency treatment when required. Now, Denplan Care is part of the AXA Group.

We have deliberately made no mention of the scale of monthly fees that you might expect to pay because these depend upon:

(a) your previous dental history and your current oral health;
(b) your possible future needs;
(c) the location of your chosen dental practice;
(d) your dentist's overheads and other costs which may also be dependent on location.

It is not surprising that a growing number of people have decided to join practice plans, such as Denplan, and, for a monthly subscription, have peace of mind about the cost of future dental care and, moreover, take part in a prevention-oriented programme of care. At the time of writing more than 1,500,000 people subscribe to Denplan. The average monthly payment is around £16, while some people pay less than £10 per month. Denplan retains a very small percentage of the premium to cover administration costs, but the bulk of your payment goes to your dentist.

THE HSA PLAN FOR DENTAL CARE

This is part of an overall package of health care which includes your dental care and treatment. It offers 100 per cent cash back for your dental examinations and treatment up to a pre-arranged annual limit. It also includes a similar cover for optical treatment (though this is not the domain of this book). you may claim
from the day your cover starts (except maternity cover). resident children up to eighteen years of age are covered for free.

Based on a family of four including two adults at £3.00 each per week, you would be covered for up to £360.00-worth of dental care, £360-worth of optical care, £280.00 per week as an hospital in-patient, and up to £800.00 for consultations. They also list eleven additional benefits which are covered, including registered physio-therapists.

In summary HSA will pay up to 75 per cent of these costs up to the pre-determined maximum.

The help line can be contacted on 0800 0854321.

Moments before going to press with this book the authors received news from HSA that in September 2006 they are to lauch a new Dental Plan. Under the banner 'Kiss goodbye to unhealthy teeth, say hello to HSA', this plan offers a wide range of benefits for both NHS and private patients. Call 0800 1070386 for details.

OTHER SCHEMES

There are many other plans, some of which cover other aspects of medical care. Some dentists have begun their own 'in house plans'. The dentist of your choice sets a fee level for you for the year and you pay so much per month. This way you budget for most eventualities. The fee level is something you would discuss directly with your dentist.

FINANCE PLANS

As dental treatments become more and more sophisticated, the cost of treatment rises and, while the decision to borrow money for any purpose is up to the individual, we mention here some additional options which are becoming increasingly available.

One such company offering finance plans is called MEDENTA. It pays for more elaborate courses of dental treatment, from £350 upwards. Medenta pays your fees to your Medenta registered dentist of your choice, and details of your repayment plan would be discussed with you by the dental practice team. Like all loans, Medenta's facilities are subject to status/credit checks. Medenta can be contacted independently on 01294 316559 and on the Internet at www.medenta.com

Denplan, mentioned earlier, also provides finance plans for dental care outside of your routine Denplan membership.

Please note that this list is not exhaustive and serves to highlight the products which become available as the face of dentistry changes.

The Hospital Services Association offers a dental insurance scheme which will cover you for the cost of treatment up to a pre-arranged maximum.

Many other organizations are entering this area and we should not forget that, although it seems unlikely at the moment, the present government or future governments may decide to commit extra funds within the National Health Service for dental care. 'Dental health is a priority concern for all nations.' said the then President of the United States, Jimmy Carter, in 1976 and we should certainly welcome a similar pronouncement by any serving British minister.

THE NATIONAL HEALTH SERVICE

At the time of writing, it seems likely that a national dental health service will continue to exist but that it may be limited to providing care for those people who, for whatever reason, are currently exempted from paying charges. We would deplore any situation in which 'ability to pay' ever over-rode the dental health needs of anyone so there must always be some state-funded scheme for those unable to pay and we must also ensure that it is in no circumstances a two-tier system.

The National Health Service was founded in 1947 and, at that time, many of the techniques used widely in medicine and dentistry today were little short of science fiction fantasy. Most people nowadays have a not-unreasonable expectation that they will receive the best, and most up-to-date care available. Such care is costly, and successive administrations, and many other people, have concluded that it would be difficult, if not politically impossible, to provide an all-embracing state scheme, paid for by the tax-payer, that could cater for the clinical welfare of a population of sixty-two million people.

CORPORATE PLANS AND 'INDUSTRIAL DENTISTRY'

Some of the insurance companies offer a 'corporate plan'. In a scheme such as this, the insurer invites a business employing a number of staff to enrol its employees en bloc and this allows the individuals to benefit from a mutual discount. Each employee can still attend the dentist of his or her choice and, of course, there is no pressure on any employee to join the company scheme.

Some bigger businesses actually employ their own dentists who work on the premises. In this way, their staff can maintain good dental health without needing to take a lot of time off work to visit the dentist. In cases like these, the uptake of this kind of dental treatment has been reported to be as much as 70 per cent whereas among the general public as a whole, only 47 per cent regularly visit a dentist. This demonstrates clearly that easy access to dental care facilities is an important issue.

11 SMILING THROUGH ... THE SHAPE OF TEETH TO COME

In the first edition of this book, Chapter 9 was entitled 'The shape of teeth to come'. Below we have included the text of that chapter unchanged as well as the text of 'An author's note for the future'. When you read through them, you will see that some of the predictions we made in the mid-1980s have now come to pass. And certainly, the advent of dental health schemes provided by companies such as Denplan, Norwich Union, and HSA has opened up a whole new way of funding dental care for many people.

THE SHAPE OF TEETH TO COME

Throughout this book, we have emphasized that prevention is better than cure in dentistry. And, for everyone concerned with health care, there should be just one hope in their minds: that prevention of disease will become a reality. We are not there yet; a lot of work remains to be done and there is much to teach the young and old. As the tide is already turning and quite quickly now in favour of the preventive approach, more dental practices will be engaging the services of dental hygienists and personnel associated with dental health education. Let us hope that augmenting the speed with which the 'dental good news' is spread is associated with an increase in employment of people trained to pass on this information. Restorative dentistry for the treatment of tooth decay is likely to remain with us for many years to come, however, and will probably always be required for repairing traumatized teeth. Remember that, as we have explained, restorative dentistry is likely to be more effective and long lasting if plaque is controlled. Periodontal tissues in particular depend on the body as a whole to remain healthy. Therefore, the concept of whole body health needs further emphasis.

As we keep our teeth for longer and longer, the jaws may tend to become more crowded so that some types of orthodontic treatment will become more common. On the other hand, as decay is reduced and fewer and fewer teeth are lost prematurely, the mouths of more young people will have the chance to develop with a satisfactory occlusion so that less orthodontic work will be required to rectify other types of malocclusions. For older people, there is hope, too. As surgery techniques improve and quicker and quicker ways of treating adults with orthodontic needs are found, people who may now feel that it is too late to bother about their teeth may have the change to enhance the appearance of their dentition.

Many factors, such as vaccine research, sugar substitutes, and, of course, the often-mentioned oral hygiene, are vital to maintain sound teeth and gums but perhaps the most important of all is a real desire, among everyone, to keep their own natural teeth all their lives. The overall importance of having good teeth and gums should be the point that is emphasized, perhaps by well-designed advertising in the media. We hope that, in future, government information services will be persuaded to promote dental health measures more frequently and more forcefully. In the UK, for example, some doctors have set up discussion groups with the help of the Royal College of General Medical Practitioners to which patients come to ask questions that might not be asked during a normal surgery consultation. We certainly believe that it would benefit dentists and patients alike if a similar scheme were to be adopted by the dental profession on an informal basis and at local level, so that many of the problems which worry patients could be cleared up.

There are still hurdles to be overcome, however. Reluctantly we have to confess that dentists themselves are sometimes a little slow to accept change. In 1973, for example, the designer Richard Satherley won the Melchett award for designing the steel mobile dentistry unit which is illustrated in Photo 23 and reproduced with his permission. It consisted of a central column which carried air, water, and electrical services and which supported three rotary storage units made of plastic-coated steel. This particular design of equipment, which would help to reduce anxiety by its appearance and give the dentist a more comfortable environment in which to work, would be welcomed. It is a pity that cost is such an important factor in the choice of dental equipment. In the United Kingdom, for example, it may be the fee structure operating in the National Health Service which discourages some dentists from choosing such equipment. Many practices are extremely well equipped but, in some quarters, there is a reluctance to update.

Perhaps when the dental profession moves away from the 'item for a fee' approach, it will be encouraged by the fee structure itself not to choose equipment primarily on the basis of cost. It is important that the dental surgery should be designed to create an atmosphere which is pleasant and relaxing. In the photograph the way in which the instruments are thoughtfully and discretely hidden on the unit should reassure an apprehensive person. If for no other reason, there should be a change in the way that dentists are remunerated for their work so that they can operate in attractive surroundings with well-designed equipment to the benefit of dentist and patient alike. The authors hope that Richard Satherley's and other effective designs will become more widespread in British dental surgeries. We have also included an illustration from the 1912 catalogue of the Dental Manufacturing Company which shows the earlier 'twentieth century chair'. No doubt you will agree that it is a most interesting item of furniture and it probably did its job extremely well at the time but methods of dental care and treatment have changed and equipment should continue to develop, too.

There are many disciplines involved in dentistry and many discoveries yet to be made. We hope this book has revealed something of the science and that there is more to it than just looking into mouths all day. We hope, too, it has shown that the dental surgery should hold few terrors for anyone, especially if they care about the welfare of their teeth and gums.

Fig. 29 The 1912 '20th Century Chair' by D. M. Co. Ltd.

Considering future trends in dentistry, we obviously hope that attitudes will change. A start has already been made and we have mentioned earlier the concept of whole body health which should include teeth and gums. On a more practical level, changes in attitude are only likely to be brought about through media publicity on the same scale as the anti-smoking campaign waged in the press and on radio and television. Bearing in mind the importance of diet on the health of the dentition, it would be a good idea if all foodstuffs were clearly marked to indicate the levels of sucrose they contain, as well as all the other ingredients, including cholesterol, for example. Of course, people in the medical professions, including midwives, nurses, and general practitioners, should all help to promote the prevention message and close liaison between these people should be encouraged.

Detecting decay

Methods of detecting decay early have depended upon a visual examination of the teeth using a dental mirror and probe which catches in any sticky areas. Radiographic pictures are taken to ensure that decalcification of the enamel has not begun at the contact points or, indeed, beneath old fillings. Even when practised by the most experienced dentist and carried out with the best possible care, these methods are not 100 per cent accurate but, no doubt, they will be with us for many years to come. Recently, however, a device has been developed that measures the electrical activity of a decaying tooth which depends upon the moisture content that is present around a carious site. Having taken a reading, the dentist refers to a chart with readings based upon a scale of 0 to 10 degrees of electrical conductivity. A figure higher than 5 indicates that a cavity is developing.

Obviously, X-ray photography will continue to be needed to investigate the condition of roots and bone but, because X-rays are potentially dangerous to dental staff and to patients, it is vital that more stringent regulations should be laid down straight away governing the use of lead aprons and protective screens for the operatives. X-ray machines in use today are extremely well designed and little scattering of the X-rays occurs but there is still no room for complacency. All dental personnel should use radioactivity measuring devices and all X-ray equipment should be checked periodically by the company that installed it or by government-appointed agencies – spot checks are not enough. A recent report, for instance, showed that of 585 X-ray machines in a random sample of practices, several fell below the safety standards of the Health and Safety Executive. (Ref. DHSS, Jan. 1979). A certificate of worthiness, we feel, should be on display to show that the X-ray machine in use in a particular practice is safe.

The same degree of priority should be given to the sterilization of equipment used in a dental practice so that there is less risk of transmitting infectious diseases. Autoclaving dental instruments is a most acceptable way of ensuring adequate hygiene but the equipment is extremely costly and this may be the reason why sterilizing equipment by this method is not more commonplace. Again, perhaps the government could assist dental practices to some extent in this important aspect.

Other methods of examining bone and dental tissue may be developed. Ultrasound techniques may have some use in ageing foetuses and recording their dental development. Perhaps we may see a method of identifying the 'at-risk' patients in terms of their susceptibility to dental disorders so that they can be advised on their particular needs for even more stringent oral hygiene.

We hope that dental disease is not in itself a precursor to other illnesses, such as the sore throat which precedes some cases of rheumatic fever. But, one never knows, and there may be a link between some systemic diseases and tooth decay or gum disease. One American professor certainly thought it was worth investigating the changes in blood chemistry that may be associated with gum disease.

Materials science has made vast strides in the last decade. The use of high-impact resins in the construction of dentures and the use of composite filling materials that match tooth colour and have desirable structural properties may mean that the grey amalgam filling and the gold crown can be relegated to the history books.

We have already referred to forensic dentistry but, as decay becomes less prevalent, the identification of human remains from dental records of those burnt in accidents, for example, will become less useful as the pattern of fillings in a given record will be absent. It is important, therefore, that tooth loss in the deciduous dentition is accurately noted in your children's records and that any minor blemishes in the first or second teeth are documented. Of course, this is your dentist's responsibility but sometimes records are lost and a knowledgeable parent may be able to save a considerable amount of anxiety for herself if she knows that, say, the child's second incisor had a deep pit in the surface.

The use of radiography is also important in forensic dentistry and a note in your diary that X-ray photographs of your teeth were taken on a particular day may well prove useful. Tell your family which dental practice you attend and record the name of the dentist that treated you.

It may be that lasers will become more widely used in soft-tissue surgery. Perhaps a silent drill would be of great benefit to patients, dentists, and assistants alike.

Computerization has already entered the dental field and probably, in the future, more and more practices will use them to assist with administration. Their use in research is, or course, most important, and showing the trends in types of treatment within a particular practice may prove to be extremely useful in monitoring the volume and types of treatment in different parts of the country.

Video games using the theme of destroying plaque bacteria have now come on to the market. Perhaps video programmes about dental health could be more vigorously promoted.

The use of fibre-optic light in enhancing the dental operator's field of vision is actually being used already, although it is not commonplace. Holograms have also been used to record orthodontic malocclusions, and this certainly has the advantage of eliminating the storage of plaster models of the jaws – quite a problem in a large practice catering for many orthodontic cases.

It is likely that the way in which undergraduate dentists are taught will change in the future, with more emphasis being placed upon dentist–patient communication techniques as well as on the pitfalls of running a dental practice as a business. Dentists and dental hygienists, too, may be instructed in deaf-and-dumb sign language and, of course, it would be an excellent idea if dental health literature was more widely available in Braille editions.

Where patients are unable to understand English, problems of communication can obviously arise. In some cases, community leaders would be well advised to seek information about dental health and arrange for it to be reliably translated into the languages concerned. Sudden alteration in dietary habits can result in dental disaster for some people and they should be alerted to this danger as soon as possible.

We are happy to end on the encouraging note, however, that a survey carried out in 1983†, showed that only 48 per cent of five-year-old children had suffered some dental decay. In 1973, the figure was 71 per cent. Improvements were found in all age groups from five to fifteen years. The most encouraging result

† Reported in *Children's Dental Health*, OPCS Monitor, 1983.

was that in six- and seven-year-old age groups, only 19 per cent of children had experienced dental decay whereas in 1973 the figure was more than twice this, at 39 per cent. We are sure that this trend will continue and hope that our book, and others in the same vogue, will assist in the process.

AN AUTHOR'S NOTE FOR THE FUTURE

From the cover on this book, you will have gathered that two authors have been involved in the writing of this book. Obviously, one of us is a qualified dental surgeon and it has been his intention throughout to develop a book which will serve to help people to understand how they can best look after their teeth, in conjunction with a dentist of their choice, and to allay many of the fears which so many of us hold about a 'visit to the dentist'. My own role as an editor and writer has been to assist in that task.

In my childhood, my own teeth, like those of many others of my generation seemed to be an endless source of pain and trauma largely because of a real lack of sensible dental education and, often, misplaced fears.

A persistent image in a nightmare which plagued me through-out my childhood and into my teens was that my mouth would suddenly become overflowing with crumbling, decaying teeth and that I could never find a dentist. I gather that 'teeth dreams' are by no means uncommon and may have no connection at all with dental problems, but it did leave me feeling that my teeth would not last me far beyond my twenties. This fear was heightened firstly by the knowledge that my mother had been fitted with full dentures by the time that she was twenty-eight, and secondly because my early experiences with dentists were far from happy ones. One particular incident that I remember only too clearly occurred at the age of eight when my parents were moving house from Wiltshire to North Devon. On the day of the actual move, which in 1957 was rather less easy than such events are today, I was suddenly stricken with searing toothache. Fortunately, then there were less pressures on a dentist's time than there are today and I was whisked off to the dentist that very morning. The tooth was removed; it was a painful experience and I did bleed rather more than I liked although, of course, the socket was plugged with a gauze pad. In this condition, I travelled the hundred or so miles in an ancient Standard 14 motor car to our new home.

Unfortunately, although the bleeding stopped, the pain didn't subside and the whole of the side of my face began to swell. Being new to the area, we did not have a dentist and, over the weekend, my face became inflamed and my temperature rose dramatically. Naturally, my parents were concerned and, on the recommendation of colleagues, telephoned a doctor. To his credit and my eternal gratitude, he arrived at 8 pm on a Sunday evening forearmed with a hypodermic syringe and liquid penicillin. I had a severe infection from the extraction. Ever since I have lived in mortal fear of having teeth extracted not, of course, that I have managed to avoid the experience again since that time. Indeed, I now have only twenty-seven rather than the full complement of thirty-two teeth, most of the molars and premolars are filled with amalgam, and two of them are crowned; a broken front tooth has been restored by acid etching and another by a cap. Not least of my fears has been that I would either lose all my teeth at an early age or that they would be so badly decayed that I would be blessed with an even less attractive appearance than the one with which I was born.

Like many post-war children, I had sugar with everything and, with the demise of rationing, sweets were the new delight to be offered as a reward for all good behaviour. Few children in small country towns were encouraged to visit a dentist unless it was with toothache, and cleaning the teeth was not the standard morning and bedtime routine that it is for most children today. All in all, hardly the best of starts for the health of my mouth and this is the main reason why I was so delighted to be involved in writing this book. Since those early days, dentistry has progressed by leaps and bounds. I actually look forward to seeing my dentist, safe in the knowledge that I can happily discuss the care and condition of my teeth in pleasant surroundings. Consequently, at the advanced age of thirty-six [note, now fifty-seven] most of my teeth are still in my mouth and look quite good. I now feel very warmly about modern dentistry and look forward to further advances in gum and teeth care.

As a lay person at the receiving end of dental treatment, however, there are still ways in which I could envisage 'the shape of teeth to come'. I hasten to add that these are only the thoughts of an interested person and may not have any place in future reality. From a position of knowledge, the senior author has already outlined the directions that dentistry and dental education may take and from which the public at large could benefit. These are possibilities and probabilities, whereas my own ideas may simply be flights of fancy.

For example, we have already discussed the ways in which

techniques have been developed to map the shape of the mouth and its development for orthodontic purposes. We have also looked at the ways in which computers might be used for tasks such as record keeping. Is it possible to link these two developments? Although considerable advances have been made in the materials that are used in taking impressions for denture and crown work, nonetheless, having an impression taken is still not a pleasant experience and does cause some people to retch. The models that result also cause some problems in finding space for storage and, in my case, I was presented with mine to keep at home in case of future need. I wonder, therefore, whether it may, at some time in the future, be possible to map the mouth by means of a hologram and store the record on a computer which could then easily be sent down a telephone line to a computer in another dental surgery should the patient have cause to change dentist. This ought to be less unpleasant and more fun for the patient and be more accurate and efficient for the dentist.

No-one is likely to go out and hire a dental hygiene video tape for home entertainment but perhaps the time spent in the waiting room could be put to valuable use if the room was fitted up with video recording equipment. Provided any films shown were carefully planned and made, the waiting period could be less boring and patients may be able to learn painlessly about the importance of dental hygiene, diet, and so on.

It seems to me, too, that, if it is not already happening, there could be room for greater liaison between the dental and materials sciences in developing new substances for protecting the teeth and for restorative work. We have already looked at fissure sealants, acid etching, the use of acrylics, gold, porcelain, and chrome-cobalt, etc. but one of today's wonder materials is carbon fibre which is flexible, light, and very strong. If it is non-toxic and can be manufactured in the appropriate colours perhaps carbon-fibre dentures may one day be available although, hopefully, by that time, there should be fewer people in need of them anyway if dental education develops in the way that we hope.

YESTERDAY, TODAY, AND TOMORROW

In *Have Healthy Teeth and Gums*, Neil Curtis speculated on the possibilities of more comprehensive labelling of foodstuffs to reveal their ingredients, particularly sugar content. This is now being implemented but it is a pity that some manufacturers have chosen to use the phrase 'no added sugar' because, although it may be perfectly accurate, some people have been misled into thinking that these products are safe for a child's teeth.

Materials science in dentistry has certainly developed rapidly and this could not be better illustrated than by the effectiveness of dental implants.

X-ray machines are now more closely monitored than in the past and the use of ultrasound in medicine has come on by leaps and bounds, although not to any marked degree in the dental surgery.

At the time of writing, so far as the authors are aware, video games have not yet found their way into dentists' waiting rooms but we suspect it may not be long before a dental company devises something along the lines of 'The Plaque Attackers'!

More and more surgeries are computerized.

THE USE OF LASERS IN DENTISTRY

The word 'laser' is an acronym for light amplification by the stimulated emission of radiation. Scientifically, this refers to a technology in which the random movements of particles of light, photons, are focused into a fine beam. If you place your hand near an electric light bulb (not too close!) you can feel the warmth it emits as well as the light. If you were to concentrate this energy output into a fine beam, the energy is enormously intensified and some laser beams are powerful enough to cut through the hardest-known materials.

At the moment lasers have only a limited use in dentistry but they would seem to offer a lot of advantages in certain dental techniques. If cavities were to be prepared using a laser beam instead of a conventional drill, there would be no off-putting whine – a marked improvement in comfort for patients, dentists, and staff alike. In addition, the rate of transmission of the pulses of energy of a laser is so high that the brain would scarcely have time to translate the pulses into a pain sensation. Indeed, although it is yet to be explained, it seems that a tooth can even be anaesthetized using a laser beam.

There is still some way to go before lasers could be used, for example, to prepare a tooth for a crown but areas of decay can be vaporized. On the other hand, lasers may offer benefits to patients suffering from sensitive teeth because the tiny exposed areas of dentine can be sealed by applying a laser beam to the sensitive area.

Lasers could also be used to seal the deep grooves on the molar teeth which, at present, are sealed using the acid etching technique described in the chapter on prevention. The target area is marked with a pencil so that the darkened surface absorbs the laser energy more readily. Overgrown gum tissue around crowns or around erupting wisdom teeth can be bloodlessly removed using a laser beam which will also stem blood flow after an extraction. Lasers can be used in root canal therapy to remove infected nerve tissue.

One particular advantage offered by laser dentistry, which is of especial interest to many dentists, is that, during a cavity preparation, the amount of contaminated spray is reduced. It seems very likely that the laser beam actually sterilizes as it cuts both soft and hard tissue. In addition, there is less need for the use of messy swabs and tissues. During any procedures using lasers, however, the operator must have eye protection and the patients should wear special goggles.

Although there have been notes of caution about the long-term effects of the use of lasers in dentistry, we might expect a further expansion in the use of this 'Star Wars' technology in future. Dentists have welcomed the media attention given to the lasers. Children are especially interested in the 'ray guns', once confined to

23 Design for dental equipment. This was the winner of the Melchett Award (*Courtesy of Richard Satherley, Satherley Design Associates, London.*)

24 and 25 (below)
Cone Beam Computerized Tomography (CBCT) Imaging System – Planmeca.
The latest innovation in digital radiography equipment makes possible the capture of all the imaging you would expect from standard Panoramic X-ray machines with the additional benefit of 3D imaging and reduced X-ray exposure.

the imaginations of science-fiction writers, while simple dental procedures can be carried out painlessly and efficiently. Lasers cannot, however, be used to remove old amalgam fillings for the mercury vapour released in the process would be toxic, so the 'old-fashioned' dentist's drill would seem not to be redundant yet.

At the time of writing a dental laser costs about £40,000 so, at the moment, they do not adorn many dental surgeries in the United Kingdom and, if these machines are used, then the patients can expect to pay additional charges.

THE LETTERS AFTER
A DENTIST'S NAME

LDS	Licentiate in Dental Surgery
BDS	Bachelor of Dental Surgery
BChD	Bachelor of Dental Surgery
BDSc	Bachelor of Dental Science
MGDSRCS	Member in General Dental Surgery of the Royal College of Surgeons
FDSRCS	Fellow of the Dental Society of the Royal College of Surgeons
MSc	Master of Science. [This may be in a dental speciality such as Orthodontics, Restorative Dentistry, or Periodontology.]
Dip. Orth. RCS	Diploma in Orthodontics of Royal College of Surgeons
FGDP RCS	Fellow in General Dental Practice of the Royal College of Surgeons

All dentists practising in the United Kingdom will be registered by the General Dental Council. The absence of a dentist's name from the Dental Register – which is available in most public libraries – may mean that the application for registration was received after that year's publication of the Register, and a record of registration will be held by the General Dental Council in London.

'Dentist', 'Dental Surgeon', 'Dental Practitioner' are all terms used to describe a dentist. In the United Kingdom, since the 'Dentists Act' was passed in 1921, it is illegal for any other person to practise dentistry. Your dentist has undergone rigorous training over a four- to five-year period in many branches of medical science, such as anatomy, physiology, and pathology plus extensive clinical training in all the surgical procedures required in General Dental Practice. All courses are university based and require a great deal of commitment from the student.

SOME USEFUL ADDRESSES

British Dental Association (BDA)
64 Wimpole Street
London
W1M 8AL

British Dental Association Scottish Office
Elmside
19 Hay Street
Perth
PH1 5HS

British Dental Association Northern Ireland Office
131 Ballygowan Road
Banbridge
BT32 3QX

British Dental Health Foundation
Eastlands Court
St Peter's Road
Rugby
Warwickshire
CV21 3QP

BDHF Helpline for anyone worried about visiting the dentist.
Telephone: 0788 546365 (Mon.–Fri. 9 am–5 pm)

British Society of Medical and Dental Hypnosis
Enquiries and Correspondence to:
Administrative Secretary
42 Links Road
Ashstead
Surrey
KT21 2HJ

General Dental Council
37 Wimpole Street
London
W1G 8DQ
This is the governing body of all dentists in the United Kingdom.

The Phobic Society
Telephone: 061 881 1937

Locally, the names and addresses of all General Dental Practitioners who practise within the National Health Service are held by your local Primary Care Trust (PCT). Dental practitioners' names and addresses may also be found in Yellow Pages and Thomson's Local Directories. Emergency services are often given in local newspapers and by NHS Direct.

GLOSSARY OF TERMS

Word in SMALL CAPITALS indicate a cross-reference.

amalgam
a mixture of silver, tin, mercury, and sometimes copper which has been used for more than 100 years as a dental filling material.

anodontia
describes the absence of natural teeth and can be partial or complete.

articular
refers to the surface where movement may occur between bones, as in joints.

bridge
in the United Kingdom, a bridge is a fixed dental appliance that replaces a missing tooth or teeth. In some countries, 'removable bridges' are referred to but in the UK, these are known as dentures.

bruxism
the habitual grinding of teeth; bruxism may be continuous or nocturnal.

buccal
the cheek side of the tooth, that is, the side of the tooth that is adjacent to the cheek muscle (the buccinator).

calculus
calcified material – debris on the surface of the tooth or denture. It can be above or below gum level.

caries
synonymous with decay.

cementum
a hard, calcified layer around the root of a tooth. The so-called PERIODONTAL fibres that attach to the bone are embedded in the cementum.

composite
a tooth-coloured filling material that may be used to restore a tooth and/or enhance its appearance. Composites are made from a mixture of tiny particles of quartz with plastic polymers.

condyle
that part of a bone that makes up the working part of a joint. In this book, the condyles refer to the two 'working' surfaces of the jaw joint. They comprise the 'condylar part' of the lower jaw. Also, they are two of the areas where continued growth of the lower jaw occurs.

corticotomy
the removal of bone between teeth to speed up

	their movement into the required position.
cyst	an abnormally present, fluid-filled cavity.
disclosing solution (and tablets)	a dye used to show up the otherwise whitish dental PLAQUE against the whitish enamel of the tooth.
distal	the surface of a tooth furthest from the front of the middle of the face.
endodontics	describing the treatment of the structures inside the tooth, that is the nerves and blood vessels; root canal treatment.
epithelium	the thin layer of cells that covers most of the body's surface and its natural openings.
epithelial	referring to the EPITHELIUM.
epulis	a swelling on the gum due to overgrowth of underlying tissues.
eruption	the passage of a growing tooth through the gum in its normal development.
exodontia	the surgical removal of teeth.
fissures	grooves and depressions on the surfaces of molar and premolar teeth,
frenum	the fleshy muscle attachment that extends from the inner surface of the lip to between the teeth or gum margin.
gemination	twinning. This occurs when teeth form so that the developing teeth fuse. It usually takes the form of one larger tooth in the place of two smaller ones.
gingiva	the gum.
gingival	relating to the gum.
gingivectomy	a surgical procedure to correct the contour of overgrown gum margins to eliminate 'pockets', that is, areas where PLAQUE can collect. The procedure can also be carried out by diathermy.
halitosis	bad breath.
keratosis	the hardening and/or thickening of soft tissue in the mouth or on the skin – that is EPITHELIAL tissue.
luxation	the total removal of a tooth by extreme pressure or trauma. Such a tooth is said to be subluxed.
mandible	the lower jaw bone.
maxilla	the upper jaw bone.
mesiodens	extra dental tissue in the midline of the mouth.
metronidazole	a commonly used antifungal and antibacterial treatment for dental infections.

occlusion in dental terms, this refers to the way in which the teeth meet when the jaws are closed. The surfaces that contact are called the occlusal surfaces. The term occlusal is reserved for the biting surfaces of the back teeth,

odontology the study of matters relating to the teeth.

odontome a collection of dental tissues in an abnormal pattern and/or location e.g. MESIODENS . The abnormal tissue may totally replace one of the teeth in the arch.

periodontium the supporting structures of the teeth, that is, bone, gum, CEMENTUM of the root, PERIODONTAL fibres.

periodontal referring to the PERIODONTIUM, e.g. periodontal disease.

plaque a natural deposit laid down on the surface of a tooth. Plaque consists of colonies of dead cells, bacteria, and a sticky component of normal saliva called mucin. When bathed in a diet rich in carbo-hydrates – especially the sugar, sucrose – the bacterial colonies change the sugar to acid and, at this stage, tooth enamel begins to disintegrate. The plaque bacteria also produce poisons that irritate the gum and cause bleeding through the resulting inflammation. This is the start of gum disease.

pyorrhoea a flow of pus – dead cells and infected material.

INDEX

Note: References to illustrations, figures and tables are in *italic*; those to the glossary in **bold**.